"Kathy has done it again! She's packed a book with great solutions and strategies that busy moms can use every day to manage hectic households. The advice, insights, and tips are practical, easy to understand, and applicable to real family dynamics. These are solutions that will make a difference in my life."

MARIA BAILEY
Host of *Mom Talk Radio*; creator of Smart Mom Solutions

"*The Busy Couple's Guide to Sharing the Work and the Joy* is a guidebook based on a lifetime of working together. Kathy and Bill Peel lend their expertise to the pages of this book, providing insight on how to love and lead each other and your family as you live and work together. One of my favorite points in the book is the importance of giving our best, not our leftovers, to the family, the most important organization on the face of the earth."

REPRESENTATIVE MARSHA BLACKBURN
(R-Tennessee)

"Whether you are a newlywed or have been married for years, this book will help fix and tighten the nuts and bolts of any family. In today's hurried society where the most basic family tasks can get left behind or left to one person, Kathy Peel provides a well-structured, direct, and practical guide for those who want to develop their marriage and family into a team that enjoys a balanced household. From cleaning schedules to party planning, Peel provides research, wisdom, and insight that will help you manage your everyday household work so you can enjoy your family!"

DR. JOE WHITE
President, Kanakuk Kamps

"Kathy Peel does it again, with very detailed and practical insights into how men and women can better manage their households and their relationships in a time that looks to be more challenging than most would expect. There couldn't be a better time to absorb the valuable advice in this book."

HARRY S. DENT JR.
Author, *The Great Boom Ahead* (1993) and *The Great Depression Ahead* (2008)

"Kathy Peel expertly lays out everything couples need to know about working together, from managing a home and finances to creating family traditions and organizing mealtimes. Insightful and extremely comprehensive, this book is a necessary resource for couples at any stage of marriage. With tools to help you and your partner manage your household and divide tasks fairly, Peel will help you and your spouse tackle home, marriage, and family as a team."

STACY DeBROFF
Founder and CEO of Mom Central, Inc., www.momcentral.com

"I work with many organizations to build winning teams, but when it comes to building a winning family team, I turn to Kathy Peel for advice. My wife and I have truly benefited from Kathy's books, and we consider this timely book a must read for anyone who feels that busyness and stress are stealing their family's joy. Thankfully Kathy gives us the tools to take on these challenges and create a strong, peaceful, and joyful family."

JON GORDON
Best-selling author, *The Energy Bus* and *Training Camp*

"Kathy Peel's newest book, *The Busy Couple's Guide to Sharing the Work and the Joy*, should be required reading for every couple seeking to work together as a team, 'moving from me to we'! As Kathy so ably describes, a great marriage takes a commitment to outgive the other person—out of love. Kathy, along with Bill's complementary advice, teaches us how to live this out in our daily, complex lives. As ones who understand and minister to our nation's military, we particularly recommend this great family management road map for each military family serving our nation in these challenging days."

MAJOR GENERAL (R) AND MRS. BOB DEES
Campus Crusade Military Ministry

"When we moved to Texas over 30 years ago, Kathy Peel was one of the first people I met. I have treasured her friendship and wisdom about family life. I love how she and Bill have worked together as a team over the years to raise three wonderful young men. She took my advice years ago to stay out of the kitchen so she could spend time helping other families. Now, years later, she is the 'master chef' of family life. Follow her recipe and turn your family into a team and your home into a nurturing, refreshing place for all."

JUDIE BYRD
Best-selling author, founder of Super Suppers, and host of *Judie Byrd's Kitchen* on FamilyNet TV; www.judiebyrd.com

"As a family physician for nearly 30 years, I have too often seen the heartache that results from spouses who do not work together as a team. So if your marriage is feeling a little under the weather or you just want to practice good family health, go to bed with this book, read it, and study it with your spouse. It will do wonders for the health of your marriage and family."

WALT LARIMORE, MD
Coauthor of *His Brain, Her Brain: How Divinely Designed Differences Can Strengthen Your Marriage*; www.DrWalt.com

"As the poster children for *Busy Couples*, my husband and I need this book. We work, travel, and raise our daughter together. Kathy's book is a lifesaver and so easy to read. I love the quizzes and charts and margin notes. For a busy person like me who really doesn't even have time to read, this book is something I can do in segments and then discuss with my husband. Kathy has an easy style of writing, and her own life experiences are totally relatable. This book is a must read for *every* busy couple!"

KERRI POMAROLLI
Actress, comedian, and author of *Guys Like Girls Named Jennie*

"Few guests on our radio show compel us to take out our pens and paper and write down every detail they discuss. Yet that is exactly what we do each time Kathy comes on the show. Just about every facet of our organized homes is from an idea or concept from one of Kathy's brilliant books. This book helps us remember that each family must be a team. We must work together and share in the family responsibilities, but we must be very careful about not keeping score. This book should be included in the registry of every engaged couple and given to those fortunate enough to make it to an anniversary without it!"

MAURA RIDDER AND MAUREEN BROWN
Radio talk show hosts, *Mom's the Word*, www.momsthewordshow.com

"No matter how good or bad your marriage is, real hope combined with a realistic plan of action to make things better is like a cool glass of water on a blistering hot day. *The Busy Couple's Guide to Sharing the Work and the Joy* is the perfect cool glass of water your marriage needs!"

TOM ZIGLAR
CEO, Ziglar

"This is a timely book for busy parents. Our media reports the American family is in the throes of social breakdown. Others contend 'family' is a dying concept brought on by greater wealth, mobility, and distractions. 'Not so quick,' says Kathy Peel! As a parent of a ninth-grade actress and 16-year-old soccer jock and wife to a professional football husband, I am passionately determined to reclaim what society seeks to destroy. Kathy's book is just the ammunition I need. When we establish our priorities through practical goal setting, managing the family together and parenting as a team, we can experience the joy of a vibrant marriage and the potential of a purposeful and fun family life."

SUSAN REINFELDT
President and founder, Liv2Giv Foundation

"Running a family is hard work and can be a lonely, thankless job. If the hamster wheel of daily chores (cooking, cleaning, laundry, carting around kids, etc.) is zapping the joy from your life, put out the welcome mat for Kathy Peel! Her wisdom, wit, and fresh insights will calm your nerves and inspire you. Sprinkled throughout the book is the male point of view, provided courtesy of Bill Peel. His insights lend wonderful perspective and will give you new appreciation for the burdens carried by the other half. Don't go another day without reading *The Busy Couple's Guide to Sharing the Work and the Joy.*"

ANN MATTURRO GAULT
Freelance writer for many national magazines and Web sites; contributor to *Unbuttoned: Women Open Up about the Pleasures, Pains and Politics of Breastfeeding*

"I have known Kathy and Bill Peel for decades and can attest that they, a very busy couple themselves, practice what they preach. This excellent book is chock-full of practical advice born of living busy lives, working and raising three children. Written in an accessible, easy-to-apply format, this advice will change your routines, get you out of your frenzy, and give you a new sense of peace and control over your schedule and your stuff. A must for all busy couples!"

AUTUMN DAWN GALBREATH, MD, MBA
Clinic Medical Director, Texas MedClinic, San Antonio, Texas

"Marriage is hard work, but Kathy provides simple tips to help manage your marriage. It's taken me almost nine years to figure out what Kathy has put together in this book. I wish I'd had this when I first got married. Now the trick is to get my husband to read it!"

MARIE LeBARON
Stay-at-home mom of three; creator and owner of www.makeandtakes.com

"Military couples are expected to accomplish the mission of family management under a variety of stressors: frequent moves, a deployed spouse, and innumerable volunteer roles. *Busy Couples* is an important tool that will help military couples find a balance and routine to overcome the everyday conflicts, which, in Kathy Peel's words, 'pave the way for a joyless existence,' empowering us to face military-specific challenges with new joy for our military adventure."

TARA CROOKS AND STAR HENDERSON
Cofounders, ArmyWifeNetwork.com

"If you think your marriage is going to be perfect, you're probably still at your reception. No marriage is perfect, but you can have an almost perfect one if you'll follow the practical and fun tips in this book. Kathy Peel, along with her husband, Bill, has created a great resource for couples who want to help their marriages not only survive but thrive. Whether you've been married one year or 50, get this book!"

MARTHA BOLTON
Emmy-nominated writer; author of over 50 books, including *Didn't My Skin Used to Fit?* and *Cooking with Hot Flashes*

"Every working couple can begin to transfer the organizational 'best practices' of the workplace to their home community, finding a lot of love and peace in their own crafted new normal. And Bill Peel's added perspective will resonate with men who value a peaceful and organized home. Kathy, you give us hope—men and women *can* know success in managing their work and home lives!"

MELINDA SCHMIDT
Host, *Midday Connection*, Moody Radio

the busy couple's GUIDE to sharing the work & the joy

AMERICA'S FAMILY MANAGER

kathy peel

with advice for men from Bill Peel

PICKET FENCE PRESS
A FAMILY MANAGER RESOURCE

An Imprint of Tyndale House Publishers, Inc.
Carol Stream, Illinois

Visit Tyndale's exciting Web site at www.tyndale.com.

www.familymanager.com

TYNDALE is a registered trademark of Tyndale House Publishers, Inc.

Picket Fence Press and the Picket Fence Press logo are trademarks of Family Manager Network, Inc.

The Busy Couple's Guide to Sharing the Work and the Joy

Designed by Julie Chen

Library of Congress Cataloging-in-Publication Data

Peel, Kathy, date.
   The busy couple's guide to sharing the work and the joy / Kathy Peel.
     p. cm.
   Includes bibliographical references and index.
   ISBN 978-1-4143-1620-8 (sc)
   1. Families—Time management.   2. Couples—Time management.   I. Title.
   HQ734.P374 2009
   640'.43—dc22
                                                      2009032536

Printed in the United States of America

15 14 13 12 11 10 09

7   6   5   4   3   2   1

dedication

*To Donald and Barbara Hodel,
who have been a wonderful example to Bill and me of what
it means for a husband and wife to love each other through
the years, for better and for worse, in sickness and in health.
Don, who served as Secretary of Energy and Secretary of the
Interior under President Reagan, says he and Barbara have had
a long-standing disagreement over who deserves the majority of
the credit for such a splendid relationship. He is convinced it is
she. She is convinced it is he. Their commitment to outgive each
other is surely one reason why their marriage is worth emulating.*

contents

Note: The titles of forms and worksheets are in italics.

introduction: getting from me to we

Here's a multipart question:

- Given the unsettled expectations of men and women . . .
- Given women's earning power and many men's desire to be with their children more . . .
- Given that an anemic national economy and a shrinking workforce are pushing Americans toward home for support and strength through unity . . .
- And given that a man and woman make a marriage covenant before God to stick with it till the end . . .

How does a couple set up to "do" family right? How do two people from two different family cultures—two different definitions of what is "normal"—forge a new and third family culture that works in good times and bad, that binds them together, and that eventually sends out their offspring as fully functioning adults? How does a man or woman go from a life of "what I like and want" to "what's best for everyone"? How do two independent people who want a healthy and interdependent family segue from 18 to 35 years of "me" to the rest of their lifetimes as a well-functioning "we"?

An estimated 2.2 million couples hope to figure that out this year. They'll walk down the aisle to what they hope is happily ever after—and spend a lot of money to get there. In 2008 the wedding industry reported revenues that exceeded—brace yourself if you have a daughter—*$50 billion*.

Plenty of planning and partying takes place before the big day—not to mention acquiring enough gifts to stock a small department store. Equipped with matching linens and the latest kitchen gear, couples feel poised to take on the world together. Nowadays, many couples wisely invest time and money in pre-marital counseling. Some take compatibility tests that point out possible areas of friction—he's an introvert, she's an extrovert; he's pragmatic, she's intuitive.

Yet despite known differences, noteworthy divorce rates, and warnings from unhappily married bloggers, all newlyweds tell each other, "We're different . . . our love is stronger. Together we can overcome any adversity!"

Couples simply don't stand at the altar and think, *Our marriage will fail.* Nope, they're thinking happily ever after.

But before long, the different preferences they each brought to the relationship begin to grate on their nerves. Conflicts arise over how, why, and when to do certain things—habits they've never noticed, routines they'd rather not give up. Although they may have found enough common ground on the big issues—faith, shared interests, life goals—to want to spend the rest of their lives together, the list of potential irritations two people bring into marriage could fill a good-size book. Yet most couples don't question or discuss the little things beforehand—and it's the little things that can eat away at a relationship bit by bit.

Before marriage, couples rarely consider . . .

- how they will each react if their mate leaves dirty dishes in the sink or throws clothes on a chair;
- how they will record shared and separate events—on a calendar, synced smartphones, or the refrigerator door;
- who will shop for groceries and prepare meals;
- who will take the recycling bin to the curb;
- who will be responsible for changing the cat litter or making kennel reservations for the dog;
- how they will decide which charities and organizations to support—and how much;
- how they will divide time among circles of friends—friends from before they were a couple, friends from after they became a couple, friends from work and the neighborhood.

So much of life involves routine matters such as these.

Then add a child or two to the mix. Who will cover 3:00 a.m.

feedings, pediatrician appointments, caregiver interviews, play-dates, preschool research, car pool pickup, and mounds of extra laundry? Potential for conflict is compounded. Unresolved routine matters can reduce romance, hinder camaraderie, become fodder for resentment, and pave the way for joyless coexistence.

It doesn't have to come to this.

As I travel and speak about Family Manager strategies that mitigate conflict and advance harmony, I meet countless couples determined to "do" family right. Many of them grew up as latchkey kids or in baby boomer families that imploded. Now that they are parents themselves, they want better—for their kids and themselves—and they've committed to working together to make it happen. My husband, Bill, and I are committed to helping them.

why 50-50 won't work

One summer morning in 2008 our determination escalated as I read an article from the *New York Times Magazine* aloud to Bill. The story was about a likable upstate couple, Marc and Amy, who are living examples of an emerging marriage model that aims to split work and home life straight down the middle. Writer Lisa Belkin explained the couple's goal this way:

> *They would work equal hours, spend equal time with their children, take equal responsibility for their home. Neither would be the keeper of the mental to-do lists; neither of their careers would take precedence. Both would be equally likely to plan a birthday party or know that the car needs oil or miss work for a sick child or remember (without prompting) to stop at the store for diapers and milk.*[1]

After finishing the article, some readers probably released a sigh and said to themselves, *Way to go, Marc and Amy—it's not easy, but it's finally fair.* No more of everything falling on one person! No, sir: every responsibility comes in equal halves. She washes colored clothes; he does the whites. One night she puts the kids to bed; the next night he does. Both have part-time workweeks. When sick kids have to stay home from school, both parents are on standby.

I penned a response to the article, but what I really wanted to do was hop on a plane to New York and give this couple a big hug and an A for effort because they are doing a lot of things right. They discuss important topics like child-rearing standards, scheduling details, and housecleaning preferences. Both value their home life, support one another, and participate actively as parents.

While I applaud their commitment to manage their family well, experience tells me they're on a dangerous path, headed for disappointment. And I don't write that lightly. Bill and I had this kind of determination when we married in the 1970s. Zealous to do family well, yet absent mentors or books on comanagement, over time we cobbled a family model from the best of what we knew: the Bible and the business world. As our home-management guidelines started to gel, our partnership evolved into a Family Manager mind-set.

Thirty-eight years of marriage, three kids, and a career in researching and writing about family management have convinced me that, day to day, an equal split will never be equal. A perfect balance of responsibilities and workload is unachievable—in reality and in both partners' perception of reality. We all overestimate our contribution: if we're doing 50 percent, we think we're doing 60 percent. Plus, a 50-50 management plan promotes legalistic score keeping and relationship dynamics that threaten to divide the family we're working so hard to protect.

In the *New York Times Magazine* article, Belkin rolled out some unhappy statistics: When both marriage partners have full-time jobs, the wife does nearly twice the housework. In middle-class homes, no matter who drives off to work, the wife also does the majority of cooking, cleaning, yard work, repairs—and child care.

Marc and Amy wanted to buck the stats, and that makes good sense. Growing up, Amy had watched her widowed mother work full time—both on the job and at home. Later she saw her working girlfriends take on pretty much the same schedule. Before she married Marc, Amy had been looking for a man willing to jettison the way it's always been done to aim for equality and fairness.

Finding a way to share life's work (and joys) as committed partners and teammates—getting from "me" to "we"—is a critical issue with which every husband and wife must grapple. In the shadow of this couple's admirable desire to create a fair and equitable division of labor, as well as thousands of other couples who are searching for a way to do the same, I hope you will see in this book that marriage is much more than a you-do-your-half-I-do-mine proposition.

A great marriage takes a commitment to outgive the other person, to do more than one's fair share—out of love, not obligation. A great marriage is made up of two people who treat one another as valued partners, who willingly pitch in, and who regularly forgive one another for being imperfect. How can you create this kind of relationship? That's what you will learn on these pages. You'll discover that in good family management, 50-50 is not the gold standard and good intentions are not good enough. If an equal division of labor were doable, husbands could carry their unborn baby for 4.5 months. If good intentions were the key, prospects for a lasting marriage would be better than 50-50, which is about what we're looking at now.

how to make this book your own

This book grew out of a desire to equip busy couples with the proven strategies and practical tools that continue to help Bill and me enjoy a vibrant marriage and strong relationships with our three grown sons and two daughters-in-law. Each chapter offers opportunities for you to personalize what you read and apply the ideas in your home in ways that make sense for your family.

If possible, work through the book with your spouse. In each chapter, Bill weighs in on issues from a man's point of view. Thought-triggering worksheets will help you and your mate communicate individual desires and frustrations, then negotiate realistic expectations and workable plans.

You can read the book straight through, or if you feel particularly stressed about one area—finances, for example—you could read chapter 1, "The Business of Doing Family," then jump right into chapter 6, "Managing Your Finances." You can work through the other chapters on a felt-need basis. And be sure to check out the list of Web resources on page 205 to fortify your relationship.

Although you will benefit from reading this book by itself, it is meant to be a companion to *The Busy Mom's Guide to a Happy, Organized Home*, which contains hundreds of nuts-and-bolts solutions for running every department of a home. The book you've got in your hands will show you how to work together as a team to implement those solutions, which will foster a loving, nurturing family culture and a smoothly running home.

But I must warn you:

1. *Don't try to make too many changes at once!* You might begin with one or two areas of your home or responsibilities, like laundry or food preparation, and branch out from there.
2. *Agree to be honest and loving about disagreements you may have about your expectations.* Let's say your mother-in-law kept a hospital-clean home so your husband thinks the kitchen should be cleaned three times a day. You, on the other hand, see the need for only one daily cleaning. Helpful worksheets will help you talk out issues such as this and negotiate a compromise you both can live with.

A strong family doesn't just happen. It's the result of a passionate commitment to shared values, family members who work as if they're on the same team (because they are), and partners who invest their love, time, and energy into building equity in one another.

Every family is flawed, but done well, family says, "I love you no matter what." Done well, family fosters a healthy love of self and others, brings out the best in every person, and advances each individual member's success. Done well, family helps members discover their God-given giftedness and learn how to share those gifts and skills with the world.

Family is a safe place to learn hard truths. It's the sacred ground for training and passing on values, customs, and traditions. It shapes our inner life and our outer citizenship. Family hands us the first chapters of our story, helps us define our roles, and prepares us to write the rest.

I'm so happy you've picked up this book; Bill and I can't wait for you to realize the benefits of doing family well, reaping dividends that will multiply across generations. Whether you've been married a few months or many years, it's never too late to begin making changes that lead to a rewarding marriage, a strong family, and a more satisfying life.

Please keep reading. A lot is at stake.

one: the business of doing family

If you've read any of my previous books, you know that the Family Manager system turns on sound business principles. Every family is an organization, and every organization needs a manager. Most often it's the mother; sometimes it's the dad. In every case, the partner who answers the high call is no autocrat. To the contrary, he or she leads by serving. He or she shares responsibility and helps individual members identify and develop their gifts and talents. In our family, Bill and I are peers and colleagues, committed to a single mission, matching values, and building equity in the Peel Family Organization. The years have shown us that the dozens of roles and tasks that constitute a household all fall into one of seven departments. (See sidebar on page 2.) Applying business strategies—such as team building, delegating, and increasing productivity—promotes efficient management of each department.

Although business strategies work wonders when it comes to the business of running a home, many people make the mistake of viewing marriage as a business transaction, a common practice in cultures throughout history. Monarchies have long used marriage as a tool to strengthen alliances and treasuries. Across centuries and cultures, women have entered marriages with dowries—money, jewels, real estate—and as part of a package deal. Take the biblical account in Genesis 24, for example. Abraham sent a servant to trade a number of expensive gifts for a wife for his son.

It would seem that we've come a long way since the days when women were treated like a commodity. The trouble is . . . now men and women both are viewed as a commodity: "He got a bargain," we say, or "She's back on the market" or "He married above his pay

GOOD TO KNOW

Being married is associated with higher self-esteem, greater life satisfaction, greater happiness, and less distress, according to the Institute for the Social Sciences at Cornell University.

The Seven Family Manager Departments

Time and Scheduling—managing the family calendar and daily schedule; dispatching the right people to the right place at the right time with the right equipment

Home and Property—overseeing the maintenance and care of all your tangible assets, including your belongings, your house and its surroundings, and your vehicles

Menus and Meals—meeting the daily food and nutritional needs of your family

Family and Friends—dealing with relational responsibilities as a parent and spouse, and with extended family, friends, and neighbors

Finances—managing the budget, bill paying, saving, investing, and charitable giving

Special Events—planning and coordinating occasions, including birthdays, holidays, vacations, garage sales, family reunions, and celebrations, that fall outside your normal routine

Self-Management—caring for your body; nurturing your mind and spirit

grade." Both partners weigh what they believe to be their contribution to the relationship against what they expect to get. Then when they marry and learn that they didn't get as good of a deal as they anticipated, they often withhold and withdraw. "He's not doing his fair share, so I'm not going to do mine." Or "She's not giving me what I want, so I'm going to withhold what she wants." Relationships that operate on bargaining terms are time bombs ticking toward self-destruction.

Although the business transaction concept doesn't translate well into family life, many other business practices do. Strategies like knowing your mission, casting vision, and creating standard operating procedures are key to building a strong family and a happy, organized home. Creating a positive "corporate culture" is important too.

Every organization, be it a small business, a nonprofit organization, a Fortune 500 company, or a family, has a corporate culture—an environment that either promotes or discourages qualities like productivity, loyalty, and score keeping. Publicly held companies typically place a lot of value on pleasing shareholders, so everything revolves around profit and the bottom line. In other words, there's lots of score keeping. This type of working environment often produces employees who feel as though they're treated like a commodity, and they often adopt a bargaining mentality: *If you don't value me, I won't value you.* Complaining and blaming become the norm. Productivity declines, company loyalty dwindles, and achieving revenue projections becomes more difficult.

At least one public company does things differently. Southwest

QUICK FIX

QUESTION: *My husband and I are both so busy that normally when we need something done, we just leave notes for one another. For instance, in the morning he might leave me a note asking me to take his shirts to the dry cleaner; meanwhile, I make up a list during the week of all the minor repairs I need him to complete on Saturday. It may be an efficient way to communicate, but occasionally one of us gets annoyed that the other just expects something to be done. How do you recommend that couples like us communicate about household issues?*

ANSWER: Use a Weekly Hit List (see page 4) to specify tasks according to the seven departments. On Sunday night discuss and list tasks you both would like to see accomplished over the next week. To designate who will be responsible for each task, use different color highlighter pens or put your initials beside each item on the list. Add items with deadlines to your electronic calendar and post the hard copy in a central location to serve as an additional reminder.

Airlines puts its employees—they're called "family"—at the top. One of their mantras is, "Happy employees make happy customers who make happy shareholders." Interestingly, Southwest is the only domestic airline to show a profit every year since 1972, one year after its inception. Recently I heard Dave Ridley, senior vice president of marketing and revenue management at Southwest, give a few examples of what it looks like behind the scenes when a company values its employees—putting "family" first.

He told of the gate attendant working at the New Orleans airport

CAUTION!

"Whenever the tissue of life is woven of legalistic relations, there is an atmosphere of moral mediocrity, paralyzing man's noblest impulses."
—*Alexander Solzhenitsyn*

FamilyManager™ WEEKLY HIT LIST DATE:

TIME & SCHEDULING	HOME & PROPERTY	MENUS & MEALS	FAMILY & FRIENDS
MONDAY			
TUESDAY			
WEDNESDAY			
	FINANCES	SPECIAL EVENTS	SELF-MANAGEMENT
THURSDAY			
FRIDAY			
SATURDAY / SUNDAY			

NOTES

during Mardi Gras who would not allow an inebriated man to board a plane. Angry because he missed his flight, the man wrote a letter of complaint to Southwest's customer relations department. After investigating the situation, Southwest responded by backing up the gate agent's decision and writing a letter to the man requesting that he take his travel business elsewhere.

In another instance, a passenger left her Bible in the seat pocket of a plane that landed in Kansas City. When a flight attendant found it, she took it upon herself to track down the passenger and mail the Bible (at her own expense) to the passenger.

During the summer of 2008, Hurricane Ike blew the Texas coast apart and crippled city infrastructure, bringing Houston and surrounding communities to a halt. When airports in Houston were finally able to reopen, Southwest told its Houston-based employees to stay home and put their homes and lives back together—a project that took weeks. To fill their vacant positions, hundreds of SWA employees from all over the country volunteered to fly to Houston to cover for their fellow Southwest teammates.[2]

So why did Southwest side with the gate agent and lose a paying customer? Why did the flight attendant go above and beyond her job responsibilities? Why did Southwest employees go the extra mile and choose to do more than their fair share to help out coworkers in Houston? It's because the Southwest Airlines culture is centered on its people first—before shareholders and paying customers.

This type of corporate culture doesn't just—*poof!*—happen. It is championed by company leaders who live out attitudes and actions like these as they go about their business. Day in and day out they practice servant leadership, creating an environment that positively influenced the attitudes and actions of employees. Most Southwest employees don't feel like commodities. They know they are loved, respected, and supported by company leaders. The result: Southwest has become legendary for its customer service and the way team members serve each other. Should it be any different in a family? Obviously not.

Southwest doesn't believe in corporate "big shots." Inverting the usual management pyramid, their managers are trained to serve those who report to them.

SMART MOVE

At least once a day, catch family members doing something *right*. Add energy to your home and relationships with praise and appreciation.

FROM THE HEART

Take some time to consider what family members are catching from you.

when life gets out of balance

Likewise, there are no big shots in a family. Everyone should feel loved, respected, and supported. Household operations should be supervised in a way that considers each family member's gifts, limitations, and proclivities, with everyone working together to create an environment that encourages members to identify and pursue their God-given callings. Jobs in a home should not be delegated according to gender or divided into an exact 50-50 split; this leads to mutual policing as much as it solves family needs. The scales of responsibility never fully balance in any family; to expect that they will only seeds resentment. Situations pop up and push one parent or another to double up here or back off there. If Mom is an accountant, Dad's domestic duties spike during tax season. Should work pull Dad out of town, Mom adapts her schedule to meet the kids' needs. And then there's serious illness.

Tyra Damm of Frisco, Texas, is the mom of Cooper, eight, and Katie, four. When she and her husband, Steve, both worked full time—Tyra at the *Dallas Morning News* and Steve at Children's Medical Center in Dallas—the Damms also split grocery shopping, bill paying, cooking, cleaning, and laundry duties. They didn't split things 50-50; they divvied up tasks according to available time and personal proclivities. When Cooper was born, Tyra adjusted her business hours for mornings at home. Steve picked up Cooper from day care and was the primary parent until Tyra got home at night. Following Katie's birth, Tyra quit full-time employment to freelance and increased her household duties. Still, when Steve walked in the door at night, he also jumped right into the chores, whether cleaning the kitchen, bathing the kids, or reading books at bedtime.

Family balance shifted overnight for the Damms when doctors diagnosed Steve's brain cancer, a grade-four tumor that hurtled him into a risky biopsy and six weeks of concurrent radiation and chemotherapy. Initially he responded well, but the treatment damaged his vision and weakened his left side so he could no longer drive (or carpool the kids to soccer practice or preschool). While the Damms once enjoyed a fluid division of labor, Tyra now ran all seven departments. Sadly, Steve passed away in September 2009. Throughout their ordeal, Tyra never wondered whether Steve would get well and compensate her for the months of imbalance. She knew that healthy families don't keep score.

What about your home? Is it a positive place to do the work of being a family? Does the environment promote going above and beyond to serve one another? What about loyalty? Do you stick up for each other in good times and bad?

Corporate culture is difficult to define because it's intangible. It's the collective state of mind of people who work at a company, so it means something different in every company. But the businesses that win a place on the various lists of Best Places to Work embrace some common "best practices" for creating a positive working environment. Consider these examples and how they can be adapted in the home.

Company strategy: On a regular basis, have lunch or coffee with randomly chosen employees and really listen to their concerns and suggestions.
At home: Make sure your spouse and children know you care about their opinions. Carve out time regularly to listen attentively to their concerns and suggestions.

Company strategy: Make sure employees have clearly defined goals, understand their professional growth path in the company, and have the tools and training they need to succeed.
At home: Make sure family members understand family goals for household tasks they are responsible for. Provide the training and tools they need to succeed.

Company strategy: Recognize and reward employees for creative solutions and doing good work.
At home: Look for ways to encourage and reward family members for exhibiting a cooperative attitude and doing tasks well.

Company strategy: Check out your own behavior. Are you the kind of person you'd like to work with? If you aren't, then hone your attitude, keep your promises, and be less critical.
At home: Ditto. Enough said.

As it does in a company, a home's working environment trickles down from its leaders—what they value, how and what they

GOOD TO KNOW

Having a husband creates an extra seven hours a week of housework for a woman, according to a study by the University of Michigan. A wife saves a man from about an hour of housework a week.

TECH TIP

Create a private Twitter account between you and your spouse. Since Twitter messages are limited to 140 characters, you can't carry on significant communication, but quick Tweets such as "Thinking of you—hope your meeting goes well" or "Pasta for dinner—then a walk?" Or "Rendez-vous after kids in bed?" can keep your hearts and minds connected.

QUICK FIX

QUESTION: *Since we married last year, my spouse and I seem to lock heads over how to do most things—both big and small. For instance, he's a neat freak who gets annoyed if I leave a pair of shoes in the living room. I think that's no big deal compared to his habit of coming home late from work without bothering to call me to let me know. On one hand, so many of our fights seem to start over relatively minor issues that I wonder if they even matter; on the other, these disagreements are really taking a toll on our marriage.*

ANSWER: You're right—many arguments that seem petty can damage the trust and camaraderie between a couple. However, they can also be the starting point of great conversations about what should be the "new normal" for your family. Each of you brought habits, preferences, and traditions from your growing-up years—most of which you view as the normal way to do things—into your marriage. Like every couple, from the newly engaged to those married for decades, you need to launch a discussion about what will be normal in your family. Somewhere between perfection and chaos, between your definition of normal and your partner's, you need to find common ground. Smooth functioning of your home and the quality of your relationship depend on this. The His Normal–Her Normal worksheets can help you communicate your individual views and desires and then negotiate your way to expectations you can both live with. (Note: A His Normal–Her Normal worksheet is included in each chapter of this book.)

communicate, and how they exhibit loyalty. A couple's attitudes and actions affect everyone who lives in their home.

This means, for example, that if building your career and making money are what you value most, relationships will suffer. If you are not willing to negotiate your standards, or if you habitually criticize, speak disrespectfully, or point out your spouse's or children's mistakes to others, you can expect similar attitudes and actions from them and a home that's a miserable place for all. No one in his or her right mind sets a goal to create such a negative environment. But it happens every day. And it could happen in your home before you even realize what has happened. None of us is exempt.

a man's point of view

family communication

Fifteen years ago Kathy and I decided to share home office space. It made sense—on paper. We would be in the same place at the same time when projects called for joint input. We could work more as a team on parenting and income-earning responsibilities. When one of us was traveling or pushing to meet a deadline, the other could cover parenting responsibilities and household tasks. Like I said, the plan looked good on paper.

Reality was a different story. Loving words and feelings morphed into heavy sighs and puckered brows. Before sharing the same space, we had both become accustomed to a quiet atmosphere when working. Now we had to listen to each other's phone calls, frustrated self-talk, and exasperated computer abuse when technology rebelled. We expected each other to know when we needed silence. I expected Kathy to cheer me up when I was stressed. She expected me to understand the importance of ambience; she wants her office to be colorful, creative, and "cute." This proved difficult since my side of the room usually looked like the aftermath of an explosion. Even worse, she expected me to drop everything to help her solve problems, and truthfully, I expected her to do the same for me. It wasn't long before the question arose: can a loving, understanding couple turn into monsters that devour themselves and their young?

The answer is probably yes. On some days if one of

GOOD TO KNOW

The Pew Research Center reports that Americans believe a happy marriage requires (in order): faithfulness, a happy sexual relationship, the sharing of household chores, adequate income, and good housing.

FROM THE HEART

The ability to defer to another person is not instinctive. Only God can help you do the impossible.

our unsuspecting offspring had wandered into the office and asked a simple question like "What's for dinner?" one of us might have snapped his head off. As tension grew palpably, one thing became clear: we needed to make some changes, because working together wasn't working.

Here we were: two reasonably sane people with at least average intelligence who understood the benefits of healthy communication and had established bound-aries about how we would communicate in the rest of our life together, but who had not stopped to hammer out the details about working in the same office. After our epiphany, we carved out some time to discuss our preferences and frustrations, and negotiate our way to expectations we both could live with. We also prayed for patience and the ability to remember that our highest calling as husband and wife is to help each other do the will of God—which sometimes means dropping every-thing to change an ink cartridge so handouts can get printed for a speech Kathy's giving. Today, except when we're in meetings or traveling separately, Kathy and I work together most of the time, helping each other with individual and joint projects—and we actually enjoy it. The days when a monster rears its head are few and far between.

No matter how much time you and your wife spend together, shared expectations and a vibrant relationship depend on setting up and then meeting communication guidelines. When a husband and wife understand how the other is wired, when they honor one another's unique-ness, and when they know that they're on the same team and committed to each other's success, their entire family can thrive.

 HIGHLY RECOMMENDED

Find some time when you and your mate can have an uninterrupted, focused conversation. (If you have small children, you may have to leave the house to make this happen. A weekend retreat is ideal.) Use the His Normal–Her Normal worksheet on page 13 to share and record when and how you learned what you consider to be normal ways of communicating. Talk about what you want your family's new normal to be.

Then get more specific. Ask each other the questions below. As you do, talk about how certain words, tones of voice, and actions make you feel. When appropriate, ask for forgiveness and graciously give it.

1. What are the little things I say that bother you the most? What makes you angry?

2. What ways do I communicate with you that make you feel appreciated? unappreciated? important to me? not important?

3. When is the easiest time to talk to me? the most difficult?

4. How can I show you more love and/or respect in the way I communicate?

5. Are there things you want to hear from me that I am not saying?

6. What is the most refreshing way I communicate? What is the most draining way I communicate?

7. What do you wish I would share with you that I have not been willing to talk about?

8. When is the best time and what is the best way to approach you about something that is bothering me? the worst time and way?

9. Do you ever feel dismissed by me when you are trying to say something important? How can I respond more positively?

10. What kind of words, gestures, or body language do I use that you would rather I delete from my vocabulary and actions?

CAUTION!

The brain is capable of thinking at a rate of 800 words per minute, making it easy for moments of stress to explode into lingering years of conflict because of an unguarded word spoken out of irritation. Remember the German proverb: Words are like bullets; if they escape, you can't catch them again.

Once you've finished discussing these questions, agree not to bring up old wounds again. Negotiate some mutually agreed-upon guidelines for how you will and won't communicate with each other. Create your own Communication Covenant on page 14 to make your guidelines "official." This will promote faster change and serve as a check when you slip back into old patterns every now and then.

increasing your chances for success

Bill and I meet a lot of people whose dreams for a vibrant marriage and happy home have gotten buried in the clutter and confusion of everyday life. They are good people. Smart people. Husbands and wives who are faithfully trying to run their households, nurture their children, care for their own parents, earn a living, and pay the bills. Yet when they stop long enough to consider where all their busyness is taking them, they feel frustrated—sometimes even desperate. They wonder how they will ever take charge of life instead of allowing life to charge right over them.

If you can relate, take heart, because things *can* change. But before change can happen, you and your spouse need to know *what* you want to change, and *how* and *when* you're going to do it. This book will help you partner in every area of your home and family life to bring about the changes you want to make.

Chapters 2 through 8 contain a wealth of practical ways to help you make positive changes in each department of your home. As you read, choose some of the strategies and tips that make sense for the age, stage, and makeup of your family. Then try a few of the suggestions. Planning and communication tools will help you personalize the ideas and pave the way to a vibrant partnership.

The ACT (Assess-Clarify-Tackle) process will help you and your spouse identify your stress points, priorities, and desires for each department, and then guide you to sensible ways to divvy up tasks and responsibilities between the two of you and your children, one department at a time. It will lead you—and this is very important—not to *my* strategies for running your household, but to *yours*.

To give you a better idea of what I'm talking about, here's a sample of the ACT process in the Home and Property department.

HIS NORMAL—HER NORMAL

family communication

Consider the conflicts between you and your spouse that stem from the different ways you learned to communicate in your families growing up. Discuss assumptions that you both brought into your marriage about "normal" ways couples communicate. Listen and learn from each other, then negotiate your way to your "new normal" for your relationship. (See examples below.)

His Normal	**Our New Normal**	**Her Normal**
Everyone freely expressed emotions at our house. I always knew when someone was upset with me and vice versa. We had it out and parted friends. I think holding back your feelings is harmful and destructive.	We will not repress anger and frustration, but we will be careful how we speak to each other. We will speak respectfully, taking into consideration the other person's feelings and how what we say might be perceived.	Anger was never expressed at our house, so I feel demeaned when you raise your voice and look angry. I believe that outbursts of anger are wrong and hurtful.
His Normal	**Our New Normal**	**Her Normal**

FROM THE HEART

"Good communication is as stimulating as black coffee, and just as hard to sleep after."

—*Anne Morrow Lindbergh*

Couple's Communication Covenant

1. _____

_____

_____

2. _____

_____

_____

3. _____

_____

_____

4. _____

_____

_____

5. _____

_____

_____

Signed: _____ Date: _____

Signed: _____ Date: _____

---

assess your stress

Stress is your reaction to the small irritations, annoying situations, or big catastrophes in life. Negative stressors rob you of joy and energy. Over time they may harm your health. They can also ravage relationships you hold dear.

Identifying your own sources of stress is important—as is understanding your spouse's sources of stress. The first step to effecting change in the Home and Property department is for each of you to rank your stress about specific household jobs and areas of your home, and evaluate your overall stress in the department. (You will do this by marking the Home and Property stress assessment on page 56.)

clarify your priorities and goals

Before you begin dealing with the stress producers in the Home and Property department, you need to know what's most important to you and your mate, and keep those priorities front and center in your mind. If you don't, you will end up living by other people's priorities, a sure path to frustration. While you and your spouse may want your home to be reasonably clean and tidy, your standards may not measure up to your best friend's—and that's okay.

Once you determine what's most important to you, the next step is to craft an overall statement that describes your Home and Property desires and goals, which should reflect your priorities. Having a vision of how your home would look and operate if this department were running at peak efficiency is key to making positive change. Keep in mind: if you aim at nothing, there's a good chance you'll hit it. The Clarify Your Priorities and Goals worksheet on page 57 will enable you to filter out the competing voices of your extended family, your friends, and our culture as a whole; determine what you and your spouse deem most important; and establish your overall desire for the Home and Property department.

tackle tasks as a team

After you assess and clarify, it's time to discuss how you and your spouse will divvy up Home and Property department chores between the two of you, and delegate chores to children who are old enough to help out.

The Who's Responsible for What? worksheet on page 58 makes this process much simpler, enabling you to assign responsibility for recurring household chores and list additional tasks specific to your family.

The amount of participation you can expect from family members will depend on their ages, abilities, and interests. Talk with your children about jobs that need to be done and those that might be delegated to them. And keep in mind that for delegation to work, you need to be clear about what you want done. Be sure to define job specifications in ways everyone can understand. For example, taking out the garbage also includes wiping out the bottom of the trash can, if necessary, and replacing the trash bag.

CAUTION!

If you, like many busy couples, are convinced that you can't slow down long enough to think about family priorities and goals because so many things are screaming for your attention *right now*, you're asking for trouble. A long date or weekend away to discuss these important topics will pay huge dividends.

Some tasks may also need deadlines for when the job should be accomplished.

As you begin to implement change, remember that any team—at home as well as at the office—will accept change better if they are:

- involved in the process
- asked to contribute their feelings, opinions, and suggestions
- told the reasons for and advantages of a given change
- respected for their feelings, even though they may oppose the change
- given appropriate and deserved recognition for their contributions in implementing the change

Team building is an ongoing process. It is not an end unto itself. It's not something you do once and it's done forever. In order for it to be successful, it has to be tweaked, updated, or changed as needed.

For the first few weeks after you've begun to work more as a team, schedule a regular weekly time, perhaps a Sunday afternoon, to get feedback and discuss how your division of labor is working. To give structure to the discussion, you might ask family members to assess their assigned tasks using these criteria:

- time of day the task was accomplished
- length of time it took to complete the task
- level of difficulty or complexity
- quality and thoroughness of work
- availability of tools or equipment needed to do the job
- necessary cooperation from other family members in order to complete the task

Listen carefully to your spouse's comments and children's input. Do you sense that you are moving toward your goals and living more in line with your priorities in this department? Encourage suggestions for improvement, and make any necessary adjustments or changes. Show appreciation for progress (even if it's small). Sometimes it is appropriate to reward completion of tasks in age-appropriate ways.

Whatever your stress level and starting point, implementing the ACT process will provide you with a personalized path for change in each department of your home.

the real business of family

Do you feel like you're drowning, barely able to keep your head above water, wondering if you've got the wherewithal to even read another page in this book? If so, may I gently but firmly remind you (as a friend would) of a truth that you cannot escape: you can choose *hard* or *harder*. Here's what I mean.

There's simply no getting around it: at times, life is hard—for every single person. Even for your coworker whose lavish lifestyle you secretly envy. Even for your friend who weighs less and looks better than she did before she had children. Even for your neighbor whose husband must have some type of super-spouse gene that yours seems to be missing. No one, I repeat, *no one* has a perfect life. There's no such thing this side of heaven.

That said, please remember this: although it's not perfect, life can be good. *Really good.* It all depends on your choices—what you allow to define your life and how you choose to respond to problems and pain. There are many circumstances in life that don't give you a choice, but there are plenty in which you do have a choice—though at times it may not feel that way.

I sure don't want life to be harder, and I doubt you do either. But if you find yourself thinking, *Change is just too hard. . . . I don't think it's worth the effort,* please don't give up! If you do, you could very well be choosing the path to harder, more painful circumstances.

I hope you can go through this book as a couple or join a study group of like-minded folks who want to strengthen their marriages and make positive changes in their homes. Or you may launch a study group yourself with other couples or friends. Even if you have to work through the book on your own, it will be worth every ounce of effort you can muster.

Another option you may want to consider is working with a certified Family Manager Coach who has been trained to help people and families—just like you and yours—implement the ideas and strategies that will help you build a strong family and create a happy, organized home.[3] One husband and wife who did this put it this way: "Working with a Family Manager Coach helped us turn the corner and was a lot cheaper than a therapist!"

Sadly, many frustrated couples head straight for an attorney's office to file for divorce. This is a very costly decision and can

GOOD TO KNOW

Every family hits glitches that hurl good intentions into chaos. Getting off track doesn't mean you've failed. It just means you need to make some course corrections.

CAUTION!

If you are in a situation that you feel requires professional help, don't wait to reach out. Seek immediate help if violence, drugs, alcohol abuse, or severe depression are involved. Many counselors, physicians, hotlines, law enforcement officials, and support groups have expertise in the problem you are dealing with. Not sure where to start? Pick up the phone and call a church for resources.

FROM THE HEART

Ask God to give you the courage to make positive changes in your home and marriage.

Draw on His promise: "Be strong and courageous! Do not be afraid or discouraged. For the LORD your God is with you wherever you go" (Joshua 1:9).

make life much harder in many ways. Whether the waves are just beginning to surge or you feel like you're close to going under, I encourage you to reach out and grab a life ring.

Throughout history, the closer that men and women lived to a subsistence level, the more they needed each other. It took everyone in a family working together to make it. Any force that threatened a family's stability also threatened its survival. Likewise, in early America, large family units were key to survival on the frontier.

The economic forces that threaten families today are different. We don't all have to labor together on the farm. But we still need to work together, helping each other survive and thrive. When one person is trying to get a new business going, his or her spouse and the kids who are old enough can offer tangible help and emotional support. When one partner (or both) loses a job, they can brainstorm about new jobs, help each other update résumés, offer network contacts, cover the home front while one of them retools skills or acquires more education, or help make space to launch a home-based business. When a family becomes cash strapped for any reason, they can lift one another's spirits by exhibiting a can-do attitude and focusing on the blessings of life instead of the problems they're facing. They can also keep discovering new and better ways to communicate and show their love in the context of a new challenge. They can get better at negotiating personal preferences and redefining mutual standards when things change. They can commit to working and pulling together for a lifetime because they are family.

While you're reading all the ideas for effecting positive change in your home, keep in mind that every family is unique. You will want to try some of the strategies in this book immediately. You'll want to tweak others to your particular situation. You'll want to skip or postpone other ideas—at least for the time being.

Whatever the age or stage of your marriage and family, the chapters that follow will help you develop your family's own "best practices" as you work together to get the seven departments in your home running smoothly and create an environment where you all can say, "Wow, it's good to be home!"

THE MOST IMPORTANT THINGS TO REMEMBER

1. A strong family doesn't just happen. It results from a passionate commitment to shared values and from family members who invest their love, time, and energy into building equity in one another.

2. Family is the sacred ground for training and for passing on values, customs, and traditions.

3. A family is an organization, and every organization needs a manager—someone with a team mentality who oversees home operations.

4. Applying business strategies—such as vision casting, team building, delegating, and leading by serving—promotes healthy relationships and efficient home management.

5. The dozens of roles and tasks that constitute a household fall into one of seven departments. Managing these areas accordingly promotes smooth operations and increased productivity.

6. Perfect balance of responsibilities and workload is unachievable in reality and in both partners' perception of reality; if you or your spouse is doing 50 percent, you'll think you're doing 60 percent.

7. Just as in business, every family hits glitches. Getting off track doesn't mean you've failed. It just means you need to make some course corrections.

8. If you and your spouse openly communicate about your family's priorities, as well as your individual preferences and proclivities, you'll be better equipped to make decisions all day, every day.

9. It's never too late to begin making changes that lead to a rewarding marriage, a strong family, and a more satisfying life.

10. Lean on God. He created the family and will give you the wisdom and strength you need to manage your household well.

two: managing your time and schedule

In 1850 Americans crawled into bed at a reasonable hour and slept an average of 9.5 hours a night. By 1910 half the country had electricity, but our recent ancestors were still breathing evenly with their eyes closed, on average, nine hours a night. By 1950, an average night's sleep decreased to eight hours. And by 2008, Americans, on average, got 6.5 hours of sleep a night.

How does that make you feel? Like a baggy-eyed statistic in a culture that never sleeps? But wait, there's more to consider.

We complain that we don't have enough free time, yet a study released in 2009 by the Council of Research Excellence reported that, on average, American adults accrue 8.5 hours of TV, computer, and cell phone "screen time" daily.

When I read reports like this, my first impulse is to grab my cords, keyboards, phones, and screens, and drive immediately to a hazardous waste dump, all the while wishing I could roll back the clock to 1850 and sleep three extra hours a night. In those days, no one had to deal with head-spinning deadlines, ubiquitous social media communities, and soul-draining conversations with customer service representatives on the other side of the world.

On the other hand, it's a lot easier to throw a load of clothes into the washer than to heat water over a woodstove, fill a washtub, scrub overalls and petticoats by hand (not to mention wring them out), and hang them up to dry. So even when my washer stops spinning, I calm down, call the repairman, and remember that I'm blessed—albeit sleep deprived—to be alive in the 21st century. But lack of sleep, too, can be fixed.

CAUTION!

Losing 1.5 hours of sleep per night reduces alertness by 32 percent, according to the American Sleep Disorders Association.

time management myths

The truth is, the top of my desk is missing in action, and for the past two weeks I've had less sleep than a new mother. Cobblers' kids go shoeless, they say. There are times when people who write about time management get no time off. As I complete the final stages of writing this book, my inner needle wavers between compulsion and panic. But I've written enough books to know that the rhythm of life will slow to a saner pace soon. Actually, it's thinking of time management in terms of rhythm that helps unmanageable people and families, like me and mine, manage the whole of life pretty well. I just wish I had realized this sooner.

I used to write a lot about "life balance." Years after I quit believing in Santa Claus and cellulite creams, I still clung to the belief that living a "balanced" life was possible. In my mind I envisioned a slender, married mother of three who had mastered a time-management system that smoothes every bump, makes every appointment, and absorbs surprises like a ShamWow. Overcommitment? Not this mom. She preheats the oven. She starts preparing in August for the holiday pageant in December. Her kids never look disheveled. Their beds are made and their rooms are tidied before breakfast. Their books stay shelved according to the Dewey Decimal System, and her kitchen is spread before her like a NASA control center. Oh, how I longed to be like her.

I've come to believe, however, that this woman doesn't exist and that the term *balance* can be misleading. Each of us is constantly (and often unconsciously) trying to maintain a sense of equilibrium between things like work and rest, productivity and recreation, contemplation and action, leading and following, giving and receiving. But since life is dynamic—always moving, always changing, and never static—we will never achieve perfect balance in any area.

This doesn't mean that we delete the word from our vocabulary and throw our dreams and desires for balance out the window. That would be denying who God originally created us to be. We long to live in a world of perfect order and balance. Instead of focusing on balance, however, I now think in terms of the rhythms of life, illustrated so beautifully in Ecclesiastes 3:1: "For everything there is a season, a time for every activity under heaven."

The Bible is rich with examples of rhythm, actually. Ecclesiastes 3 describes a time for planting and harvesting, a time for building and tearing down, a time for war and peace. In Exodus 20, God commands us to honor the Sabbath, a day of rest after six days of toil. Leviticus 25 describes God's plan for a jubilee year that comes every half century, a time of rest for servants and a time to return to family.

Since rhythm was so important to God as He created the world—complete with a waning and waxing moon, oceans with predictable tides, a sun that rises and sets every day, four precise seasons—there's certainly reason to look at the days, weeks, and seasons of family life and responsibilities through the lens of rhythm as well.

Contemplating rhythm naturally led me to think about music and how a concerto or any piece of music would be unpleasant, not to mention boring, if the score contained nonstop chords with no rests or variations in the rhythm. A sonata's robust first movement is usually followed by a slower, more peaceful second movement before the next movement picks up the pace again. Though each is unique, all movements continue to carry the theme and melody. They all add depth and meaning to the music and heighten enjoyment for the audience.

Consider the rhythm of your own life. What is the rhythm of your job? If you're a teacher, you do much more than teach. You gather, prepare, study, observe, evaluate, record. Those tasks all fall within the rhythm defined by the school calendar and the school day.

What about the rhythm of your home? As a parent, you constantly adjust with the seasons of your children. In the first two or three years, your sleeping patterns are defined by your child's. Just when you think you'll never get a night of uninterrupted sleep, your child sleeps through the night, not crying or leaving his room once in 10 hours. As your baby grows up, she joins a soccer team, and again your rhythm alters, this time to weekly practices and games. You learn to adjust mealtimes and anticipate traffic jams along new routes.

When you recognize that there are varying rhythms to life, you're more likely to adjust with a can-do attitude. Part of that recognition is preparation. If there are predictable times of extra stress in your life (in March if you're the mom of a baseball player, just before tax season if you're an accountant, a few weeks before grades are due if you're a teacher), take steps to make life easier for you and all the other members of your family.

SMART MOVE

Around the dinner table one night, launch a lighthearted brainstorming session. Decide what each family member's theme song might be. A cheery child's song might be "Don't Worry, Be Happy." If Dad is always under the pile, the Beatles' "Help, I Need Somebody" might be appropriate. If your family decides your theme song is "Flight of the Bumblebee," you might take that as a hint to slow down.

preparing for extra-busy times

- *Get your body ready.* Try to catch up on your rest and perhaps even sleep a little more than usual. Eat healthy meals and snacks, and don't skip your vitamins or exercise routine.
- *Plan meals that don't take a lot of preparation.* Stock up on nonperishables and supplies.
- *Plan for the fast-paced rhythm and then reward everyone.* Do something special with your spouse or as a family before a busy time at work, and plan something you all can look forward to when you finish.
- *Don't add anything unnecessary to your schedule.* Wait until the crunch is over to get your teeth cleaned or get bids for painting your house.
- *Plan your wardrobe.* Make sure everything you plan to wear is clean, mended, and pressed.
- *Communicate.* Schedule time with your family to discuss upcoming family events, and how details and transportation will be handled when you're not available.
- *Delegate.* Find a responsible teenager who'd like to earn some extra money by helping you out with errands, pet care, or other miscellaneous tasks. Check with a local high school, religious organization, or your neighborhood association for recommendations.
- *Save the moment.* If you must miss a child's performance or game, ask a relative or friend to stand in for you and record the event so you can watch it later with your child.

time management truths

In the face of overwhelming evidence, I finally accepted that the mom I dreamed of becoming was a myth. Yet as I let go of my dream, I held on to three time-management principles that had emerged as truth.

1. **There is no faultless daily planning system.** You won't discover a time-management method that will run your family's schedule with the precision of a German clock. This truth doesn't remove plaque or eliminate permanent rug stains, but it does set you free.

2. **No system is perfect, but having no system at all is insane.** Despite the absence of a foolproof process, you still have to manage your home, family, and multidimensional personal life. When this second truth hit me like a bat rolling off my middle son's closet shelf, I cobbled together my own time-management method. I devised the Daily Hit List and implemented lots of shortcuts and time-saving solutions. I draw on all these tools to determine my priorities and use time wisely.

3. **You can plan, but you can't predict.** Toilets overflow. Babysitters cancel. Sidewalks break front teeth. Out-of-town trips come up. Elderly parents have crises. Kids need you *right now*.

   Time management is about priorities: yours. Not your mother's, your best friend's, or your boss's. Only you can determine your "first things," so you'd best know what those are, lest you adopt someone else's—which may reflect values that don't matter to you a lick. If you've never considered whether you're truly living by your priorities, I encourage you to consider your answers to the following questions:

   What matters most to you?
   What quality of life do you want for you and your family?
   What kind of relationship do you want with your husband?
   What values do you want your children to embrace?
   What memories do you want them to take when they leave home?
   What dreams do you have for the distant and not-so-distant future?

It's easy to bypass the important for the urgent, especially when dishes in the sink look like a science experiment, your neighbor's on hold while you answer another call, evening meals are down to microwave pasta, and the ironing basket is overflowing. But a talk with your husband about an issue at work is far more important than a shiny sink. Listening to your daughter practice her book report outweighs listening to your neighbor recap today's *Oprah* show. Helping your son finish his bug collection should take precedence over the ironing. (In my mind, most anything takes precedence over ironing.)

SMART MOVE

Use a Daily Hit List. Selectively choosing each day what you will *do*, *delete*, and *delegate* in each department will help you manage each day's tasks and alleviate stress. To download free Daily Hit Lists, go to www.familymanager.com.

GOOD TO KNOW

In the United States, about 84 percent (27 million) of moms with at least one child under 18 years old spend time online, reports Nielsen NetRatings.

CAUTION!

Avoid extremes. A micromanager likes precise rules and routines about how things are done. She (or he) is keen on punctuality, and if you're tardy you pay. On the other hand, a macromanager might have trouble getting her family around the table because dinnertime (and perhaps dinner itself) is often a surprise. The trick is to establish routines that enable your family's schedule to run efficiently while allowing for flexibility and spontaneity.

Time management is also about *using*, not just spending, the minutes of our days. Just as we can't manage monthly cash flow effectively unless we know where our dollars are going, so we can't manage time effectively until we know where our minutes are going. Often those minutes are taken up by nonpriority activities and relationships.

time robbers

Truth is, most of us are robbed of valuable time every day, not by burglars or con artists, but by people and circumstances we unconsciously (or consciously) allow to steal our minutes. Take Malia, a woman who rushed into a Family Manager workshop in a local bookstore 10 minutes before it was over. After my presentation, she stayed until the crowd had dispersed, and apologized for being late. I could tell she wanted to talk, so we sat down in the front row and she told me about her day.

First thing that morning, she realized she'd misplaced her car keys, which made her 10 minutes late for work. On her lunch break she went to the bank to make a deposit, only to discover that in her haste to get to work, she had forgotten to put the checks she planned to deposit in her purse. After work she had to stop at the grocery store, where she wandered around until she could find something for dinner that looked appetizing and could be prepared quickly. By the time she got home, she was exhausted—not to mention concerned that some checks would bounce because she hadn't made the deposit. As she put away the groceries and started dinner, she noticed the advertisement for my workshop, which she had posted on her refrigerator door.

About that time, her 12- and 13-year-old daughters were dropped off by a neighbor with whom she shared play rehearsal car pool duty. She gave her girls a hug and made them a plate, then jumped into her car and drove as fast as she could to the bookstore. When she finished telling me about her day and why she was late, she said with relief, "I'm just glad my husband is out of town this week because, knowing him, he would have given me one of his time management lectures . . . and I would have ended up crying."

As it happened, she ended up shedding a few tears anyway when she told me how she wanted to do a better job of managing her time because her frequent mishaps and her husband's lectures were harming their marriage.

Since Malia had missed most of the workshop, I shared the concept of time robbers, those unplanned, unnecessary interruptions that steal valuable minutes from more important tasks. Using specific details from her day, I illustrated some ways she could weed many of them out of her daily schedule. She agreed to try the following solutions:

- Get up 10 minutes earlier to allow for schedule snafus.
- Install a hook near the door where she would always hang her car keys.
- Put a shelf or table next to the door where she would put the items she needed to take with her—dry cleaning, shoes to be repaired, movies to be returned, checks to be deposited—that day. (I also explained how signing up for direct payroll deposits and online bill paying could save her time and frustration.)
- Plan menus as a family on Sunday nights and make a grocery list. Ask her husband to do the grocery shopping.
- Post weekly menus on the refrigerator so whoever arrives home first could start dinner. Malia would also dust off the slow cooker and start some dishes in the morning.

Notice that we first identified those avoidable hassles that were eating up time that could have been used on more important tasks. Next we came up with a plan to address the root of each problem. As Malia discovered, sometimes that means designating a place for easily misplaced items; other times it means planning ahead; and sometimes it requires that you and your spouse hold one another accountable for how you use your time. To come up with an individualized plan for your own home, see Identifying Time Robbers on page 28.

After plotting a strategy to eliminate her biggest time wasters, Malia and I talked about a plan for the coming weekend. The girls were leaving for a church retreat Friday after school, and her husband was scheduled to arrive home from his trip around five o'clock. She shared that her husband often complained that she never made time for him, so she agreed that this was a perfect opportunity to orchestrate an evening when she could tell him of the changes she'd begun to make while he was gone. (She would install the hook for her keys

SMART MOVE

Start the routine of taking regular walks with your spouse. Even if you can walk for only 15 minutes twice a week, make it happen. Talk about how your weekly activities are fitting in with your priorities, as well as what you might need to change or adjust.

Identifying Time Robbers

Managing the minutes and hours of your day wisely is key to lowering the stress level in your life and creating a smoothly running home. Check any of the following statements that apply; then estimate the amount of time you spend on these activities each day. Ask your spouse to do the same. Discuss how you can work together to reclaim some time for things that matter most to you. Write your solutions in the space below the list.

TIME ROBBERS	TIME SPENT	
	his	hers
I answer the phone every time it rings.	❑	❑
I frequently check my BlackBerry/iPhone/PDA.	❑	❑
I am constantly picking up family members' belongings.	❑	❑
Time gets away from me when I'm reading e-mail.	❑	❑
I spend a lot of time shopping on the Internet and/or blogging.	❑	❑
At times I forget where I put my car keys and/or glasses.	❑	❑
I often buy birthday gifts and wrapping supplies at the last minute.	❑	❑
I go to the ATM more than once a week.	❑	❑
I can't get the kids to focus on getting dressed and ready for school.	❑	❑
I often run late because I can't figure out what to wear.	❑	❑
When I need stamps or office supplies, I often run out to buy them.	❑	❑
I regularly referee kids' arguments over toys and/or computer time.	❑	❑
It seems I'm always looking for the mate to socks or gloves.	❑	❑
I go to the grocery store two or more times per week.	❑	❑
I spend a lot of time stuck in traffic.	❑	❑
I can't find the bills when they need to be paid.	❑	❑
I watch TV for two or more hours a day.	❑	❑
I look up the same phone numbers over and over.	❑	❑
I usually have to call for event details because I can't find the invitation.	❑	❑
I often need to return purchased items and have to search for receipts.	❑	❑
I write the same information over and over—babysitter instructions, grocery lists, travel lists, emergency medical forms.	❑	❑

Other: _____

Other: _____

Other: _____

ACTION STEPS TO ADDRESS OUR TOP THREE TIME ROBBERS:

1. _____

2. _____

3. _____

and move a bookcase near the door by Friday.) She would also talk about more changes she wanted to make to be a better manager of time—with his help, but preferably without his lectures. She would strive to broach this topic with an attitude that revealed her sincere desire for the two of them to grow in love, respect, and intimacy and to work together to build a happy home.

Postscript: A few months later Malia reported that both she and her husband had made progress and were reverting back to their old patterns less frequently. And when they did, they talked it out, regrouped, and got back on track to becoming the husband and wife they wanted to be.

take control of technology

During the course of a day, many things can sidetrack us and gobble up minutes, but one of the biggest culprits is technology. Don't get me wrong. As I said before, I love living in the modern world. My friend Erin can see and talk to her son in real time via computer almost every day while he's stationed in Iraq. How awesome is that! Right now I'm hurrying to finish this paragraph so I can check text messages on my phone and learn if Bill arrived in Denver and our son James arrived in Austin safely. And before going back to work, I might also make a move in a Scrabble game I'm playing online with our son John, who lives 100 miles away.

The problem is, instead of using technology to better manage our time, it often ends up managing us, thus robbing our time. If we decide to quickly check our e-mail and notice messages that call for our response, it's easy to shift our focus and time—no matter what other projects we're in the midst of—to responding right then. We become like Pavlov's dogs. In the same way Ivan Pavlov used a bell to make dogs salivate in anticipation of a meal, our cell phone tweets, computer chimes, and BlackBerry buzzes have trained us to stop what we're doing—even when it's something important— to find out who's looking for us or what other people are doing. Truth is, time management is really about self-management.

tips to tame technology at home

1. Be willing to work with your spouse to establish limits on the use of work tools like laptops and BlackBerries at home.

GOOD TO KNOW

The average child today spends 45 hours a week with some form of media, according to Common Sense Media, compared with just 30 hours in school.

FROM THE HEART

It seems like yesterday I was riding herd with three active boys. I remember an older mom telling me to cherish each day because children grow up so fast. Many days I thought to myself, *Not fast enough!* I regret those days because now I know she was right.

2. Keep your home computer out in the open. Not only will it allow you to monitor your kids' usage, you and your spouse will be less likely to spend inordinate amounts of time on it if family members are nearby.

3. Turn off your computer when it's not being used. You'll be less likely to think, *I'll just take a minute to check my e-mail* if you have to restart the computer to do so.

4. Turn off your home computer at the same time each night. At the end of a long day, it's often easier to mindlessly surf the Internet than to get ready for bed.

5. Set—and enforce—limits on the time your kids spend watching TV and playing video games. The American Academy of Pediatrics recommends that children spend no more than one or two hours with any form of media each day.

6. Honestly assess whether you're relying on computers or video games to keep your kids busy so you can work around the house or get needed downtime. If so, talk with your spouse about how you can spend more time interacting with your kids and how you can encourage them to occupy themselves—whether by playing outdoors or by doing chores for extra spending money.

QUICK FIX

QUESTION: *Our computers and phones consume too much of the family time and couple time in our house. How can we control this?*

ANSWER: In order to connect with your kids and with each other in significant ways, you've got to disconnect from the world. Keep a timer by your computers to keep track of how long you're online. Just like when you're on an airplane, agree to turn off all electronic devices for a certain amount of time each night and on weekends. And remember Pavlov's dogs: don't automatically answer the phone or respond to a text message. Talk and respond to people when it's convenient for you.

a man's point of view

managing your time and schedule

My grandfather was a dispatcher for the Southern Pacific Railroad. He sat in a tall building that towered over a busy rail junction and directed rail traffic in the Central Texas corridor. Today that same job is performed from Denver via computer by one person who manages rail traffic over a much larger area. When I visited this office, I was amazed at how efficiently every car was moved along the right path to the right place at the right time—all from 1,020 miles away.

That's really what the Time and Scheduling department is about: getting the right people to the right place with the right stuff at the right time—while maintaining some degree of sanity. How hard could that be? Well, a lot harder than I once thought. Prior to my enlightenment, the way I saw it, if people living in the modern world were advanced enough to direct freight trains from a thousand miles away, surely our family of five could get to church on time. So I would pull out the car and honk the horn on Sunday mornings to remind Kathy and the boys that it was time to leave. Not the best way to get everyone in a worshipful frame of mind.

Though I'm often slow on the uptake, I do eventually learn, and in this case I learned that being the "dispatcher" for a busy family is no small task. When our three boys were school age, our home often felt like Grand Central Station. Maybe you can relate—or maybe you can't because you leave for work early and return after bedtime. Sadly, I've known men who intentionally schedule their lives this way in order to miss the chaos. One word comes to mind for a guy who does this: *chicken!*

During most of our boys' growing-up years, I worked from our home and got to see the cars switching tracks firsthand. One year they had to be dispatched to three

FROM THE HEART

The end goal of all time-management strategies is to make time for the things that matter most. Material things, commitments, and relationships all take time. Some are worth the time; others are not.

SMART MOVE

Decide as a family to calculate the amount of time involved before saying yes to invitations and opportunities. Seemingly small things—Scouts, sleepovers, bake sales, dinner meetings—can keep you from your priorities and produce a frenetic lifestyle.

different schools, six different sports practices, plus one piano lesson, two youth group meetings, and Scouts. That was the year we succumbed to purchasing an oversize SUV for Kathy. This made carpooling more pleasant for her, but it didn't make life less hectic.

When you consider the Family Manager's task of directing traffic for a busy family, you can see the importance of running this department well. How each 24-hour day is managed makes the difference between a household in constant uproar and one that hums along smoothly. Getting this department under control will reduce daily stress and free up time for the things that really matter to you and your family. If you don't control the minutes of your day, someone or something else besides you will run your life. One day you'll wake up and realize you've been rolling down the wrong track.

Consider these four points and how they might reduce stress and help your family avoid Time and Scheduling train wrecks at your home.

1. **Decide what's important.** Managing time is about deciding what's most important and determining not to let nonpriorities crowd out those things. What's most important to you? Do your wife and/or children complain about your schedule? the family's schedule? What are you not doing because of time restraints? If saying yes means saying no to something more important, say no.

2. **View time as a limited commodity.** We all have a certain amount of time—24 hours each day—and when it's gone, it's gone. It's silly to ask, "Where did the time go?" It didn't go anywhere. You spent it. Better questions to ask yourself would be, *Am I spending my time doing what I really want to accomplish according to the priorities I've set?* and *What will I not have time for if I'm spending time doing this now?*

3. **Identify your time robbers.** Think about activities, situations, or people that could be stealing minutes from your day. Did you spend too much time on the

phone, watch more TV than you thought you did, surf the Internet shopping for a boat you can't buy right now anyway, or spend a lot of time in the car, stuck in traffic, because you didn't leave the office before rush hour? Lost minutes add up to lost hours, and lost hours add up to lost days.

4. **Set up time-saving routines.** There are a lot of jobs, large and small, that have to be done to keep a family running. A lot of those jobs can fit into routines that keep you from having to waste time reinventing the wheel when everyone's wondering what's for dinner or who's going to take the kids to school.

 HIGHLY RECOMMENDED

Block out some time to discuss the family schedule with your wife. Use the His Normal–Her Normal worksheet on page 34 to get a better understanding of how you both view time. What are her key time-related stressors? Are there some things you could do—maybe some things she has asked you to do in the past—that might lessen her stress? Like getting up a little earlier so you can help get the kids ready for school? Like not checking your Black-Berry every three minutes when you're with your family? Like not automatically turning on the TV when you walk in the door? Completing this exercise with your wife is a practical way to show love to her.

say yes to what matters most

Another reason many women feel as if they never have enough time is their reluctance to say no to any request—whether out of their fear that they might disappoint someone or that they might appear less capable than their peers. The season that I learned the importance of saying no is particularly humbling to recall. My pace accelerated from blend to puree when our older boys entered the every-sport-every-activity-every-time stage, and Mom and Dad

TECH TIP

If you have an iPhone, check out the apps designed to help parents with a number of tasks. Included in PCMag .com's best iPhone apps for parents are:

- Remember the Milk: This popular list-making and task-management Web site has a mobile app to help keep tasks and schedules organized when you're on the go.
- Sit or Squat: When your child needs to use the restroom, this app gives you the nearest bathroom options, as well as stats on cleanliness, changing tables, and handicap-accessible facilities.
- Good Food Near You: When you're in the car and the kids get hungry, this app helps you find health-conscious options in your vicinity.

HIS NORMAL—HER NORMAL

time and scheduling

Consider the conflicts between you and your spouse that stem from the different ways your families managed the daily schedule when you were growing up. Discuss assumptions that you both brought into your marriage about "normal" ways individuals and families manage the minutes of their days. Listen and learn from each other; then negotiate your way to the "new normal" for your family. (See examples below.)

His Normal	**Our New Normal**	**Her Normal**
My father was an executive, and my mother was an accountant. We ordered a lot of take-out food and rarely ate dinner together, especially between February 15 and April 15. I don't want to be like my parents, but I believe that families need to flex with the demands of work.	We will make family time a priority and aim to eat dinner together three to four times a week. On Sunday nights we will go over our schedules and talk about our expectations for the coming week.	My dad worked for the postal service, and my mom taught school. We were a busy family, but everyone was home by 5:00. I believe that eating dinner together every night and having family time is a top priority.
His Normal	**Our New Normal**	**Her Normal**

were readjusting to the nonnegotiables of a small baby. My hours careened between ball games, practices, pediatrician appointments, community volunteer activities, women's ministry meetings, and nursing. I became a do-it-all-aholic. As I crammed too many things into a day, tasks like paying bills, making sure we had milk for breakfast, carpooling after school, and taking care of myself began to slip through the cracks of my daily schedule. Finally my body rebelled, and I landed in a hospital.

After a dozen medical tests, my doctor wrote on my chart: chronic mononucleosis syndrome. Today's term is chronic fatigue syndrome. This condition leaves you feeling as if energy drains out of you like water from a broken pipe, and your ability to think clearly is a muddy memory. Nonetheless, during the six hours of wakefulness to which my days were reduced, I tried to think. *How did I get here?* Because air traffic control at LaGuardia Airport was a playdate compared to my daily schedule? Because my lips could not shape into the word *no*? Because I got up before the sun to check through a list that was all commitment and no self-care or joy?

Yes, yes, and yes.

There's more, and I don't like telling this, but it's true. When I wasn't a meeting machine or a full-service friend, I wasted my time in purposeless shopping and needless extended phone chats.

But now from my position on the family room sofa, staring at the ceiling, I contemplated how I might, should the golden hours of a full day ever be restored to me, live more wisely. One thing: I would not pass time or merely spend it. If I ever peeled myself off the sofa, I would see each day, each hour, as a gift from God given to me to become the person He created me to be and to fulfill the purpose for which He created me. I would rethink what being a follower of Christ, a devoted wife, and a loving mother meant to my daily schedule.

When a new request came in—a friend's decorating project, a neighbor's Tupperware party, or a bake sale—if it would nudge out a priority, it didn't make it on my schedule. Help organize the silent auction? Let's see . . . um, no. Sorry, I have a conflict. (Subtext: my family gets the best of me.)

It was one small step for me, and one giant step for everyone in my immediate universe. So this was the sense that came with doing the right things for the right reasons. And . . . stop the presses: when

CAUTION!

Kids are not the only ones who have to battle peer pressure. Sometimes it's hard to say no to requests for good things. Honestly think about why you are involved in so many extra activities. Do you have to teach Sunday school *and* serve on the missions committee? Do you have to be in charge of your neighborhood's annual garage sale?

GOOD TO KNOW

We will never "find" time for anything. If we want time, we must make it.

FROM THE HEART

Failing to take time to care for yourself puts not only you but also the people you care about at risk. An exhausted and deflated wife, mother, daughter, and friend is not much good to anyone.

QUICK FIX

QUESTION: *Jobs often take longer than I think they will. At the end of the day, although I'm exhausted, I realize that I haven't accomplished the most important things I needed to do—not to mention I haven't done anything for myself.*

ANSWER: Three things will help:

- Get highest-priority tasks done first. This is the best assurance that important things won't be crowded out by urgent things and other projects.

- Schedule backward. Pinpoint the time something needs to be accomplished and work backward to determine how much time you'll need to make it happen. Always add in extra time for glitches and interruptions.

- Don't overschedule your days with back-to-back tasks and commitments. Build in buffer time between activities, and take time for some things that refresh you. Just taking 10 minutes to get a little further in a novel, walk around the block, or close your eyes and listen to your favorite music can energize you for the next task.

I said no, the person who had made the request found someone else. To my amazement and chagrin, projects and meetings rolled right on without me. Events without Kathy came and went, and still a good time was had by all. The payoff for my family was this: they now got my best, not the leftovers.

If any part of my story hits a nerve, finish reading this paragraph and then close your eyes. Imagine your days spent doing what you deem most important. Imagine the clock is not the enemy. Imagine you've learned to say no, and to your surprise, it feels really good. It feels authentic. It feels invigorating. Within days, the things that improve your hours have begun to improve your family members' lives.

Eyes open now? Then get going on the ACT process and discuss with your spouse how to make time work for your family.

THE MOST IMPORTANT THINGS TO REMEMBER

1. The end goal of time management is to make sure you have time for the things that matter most.

2. Good managers of time are neither micro-managers nor macromanagers. They establish routines that enable the family schedule to run efficiently while allowing for flexibility and spontaneity.

3. Just as you can't manage monthly cash flow effectively unless you know where your dollars are going, so you can't manage time effectively until you know where your minutes are going.

4. Managing time is about deciding what's most important and determining not to let nonpriorities crowd out those things.

5. Getting highest-priority tasks done first is the best assurance that important things won't be crowded out by seemingly urgent things.

6. There are many circumstances in life about which you don't have a choice, but there are plenty in which you do—though at times it may not feel like it.

7. You will never "find" time for anything. If you want time, you must make it.

8. Time management is really about self-management.

9. There is no such thing as unimportant time. Every minute is a gift.

10. When you say yes to something, you're saying no to something else. Don't let it be your family.

time and scheduling department

Take a few minutes to think about the key causes of stress in the Time and Scheduling department of your home. You and your spouse should use a different color pen or pencil to circle the number that best describes your individual stress level for each topic.

Key: 1=No Stress; 5=Very Stressful (0=Not Applicable)

Daily schedule/routines	0	1	2	3	4	5
Morning routines	0	1	2	3	4	5
Afternoon routines	0	1	2	3	4	5
Evening routines	0	1	2	3	4	5
Bedtime routines	0	1	2	3	4	5
Kids' activities	0	1	2	3	4	5
Being on time	0	1	2	3	4	5
Car pools for kids' activities	0	1	2	3	4	5
Errands	0	1	2	3	4	5
Schedule conflicts	0	1	2	3	4	5
Work/rest balance	0	1	2	3	4	5
Time for housework	0	1	2	3	4	5
Time for paperwork	0	1	2	3	4	5
Time spent with kids	0	1	2	3	4	5
Time spent with spouse	0	1	2	3	4	5
Time for self	0	1	2	3	4	5
Television/computer time	0	1	2	3	4	5
Procrastination	0	1	2	3	4	5
Daily planning	0	1	2	3	4	5
Living by priorities	0	1	2	3	4	5
Other _____	0	1	2	3	4	5
Other _____	0	1	2	3	4	5
Other _____	0	1	2	3	4	5
Other _____	0	1	2	3	4	5
Other _____	0	1	2	3	4	5
Other _____	0	1	2	3	4	5
Other _____	0	1	2	3	4	5
Other _____	0	1	2	3	4	5
Other _____	0	1	2	3	4	5
Other _____	0	1	2	3	4	5

time and scheduling department

Your Priorities

Look again at the items in the previous chart that you ranked as a 4 or a 5. Then you and your spouse should read the "I want" statements below and place a check in the box next to the ones that best describe your priorities for managing the Time and Scheduling department in your home. Circle two or three that you each deem most important.

I want ...

his	hers	
❑	❑	to see every hour of every day as a gift, not to be irresponsibly *spent*, but *used* in a purposeful way.
❑	❑	to learn to use small blocks of time to accomplish big tasks.
❑	❑	to stop wasting time on meaningless activities.
❑	❑	to arrange our schedule so we can be on time to school, work, practices, and appointments.
❑	❑	to make decisions about how I spend my time by what's important to me and my family, not according to someone else's priorities or desires.
❑	❑	to think and plan ahead so as to eliminate as much chaos and stress as possible from our daily life.
❑	❑	to schedule time for things that I deem most important to my family and me.
❑	❑	to go to bed earlier.
❑	❑	to get up earlier.
❑	❑	to regulate our family's schedule so that we spend more time communicating and enjoying each other.
❑	❑	to learn to say no.
❑	❑	to stop procrastinating.
❑	❑	to build buffer time into our daily schedule to reduce stress.
❑	❑	_____
❑	❑	_____
❑	❑	_____
❑	❑	_____

Your Goal

Consider your individual and shared priorities, then write an overall goal that reflects your desires for the Time and Scheduling department. For this purpose, think of a goal as a broad, general, timeless statement that describes your overall aim for this department. Sometimes it is helpful to begin by identifying the key words that you'd use to describe this department when it runs well. Here's an example:

> **Key Words:** *peaceful, not rushed, on time, more time for fun as a family*
> **Goal:** *To use the minutes of our days wisely so that our days are peaceful and not rushed, we arrive places on time, and we schedule time for family fun each week.*

Key Words: _____

_____

Goal: _____

_____

time and scheduling department

Using this worksheet, divide up responsibilities for the Time and Scheduling department.

Who's Responsible for What?

Responsibilities	Who does it now?	Who else could do it?
Oversee family calendar	_____	_____
Coordinate children's/parents' schedules	_____	_____
Make dental and doctor appointments	_____	_____
Schedule after-school activities/transportation	_____	_____
Coordinate car pools	_____	_____
Orchestrate morning schedule	_____	_____
Orchestrate evening schedule	_____	_____
Prepare for future events	_____	_____
Help children manage their time	_____	_____
Secure babysitters	_____	_____
Deal with bedtimes and curfews	_____	_____
Respond to invitations	_____	_____
Coordinate rides for children to special functions	_____	_____
Plan children's schedule on school holidays	_____	_____
Plan children's schedule during summer break	_____	_____
Schedule appointments for elderly parents	_____	_____
Implement time-saving routines	_____	_____
Coordinate time-off requests for work with spouse	_____	_____
Meet deadlines for team sports registrations	_____	_____
Meet deadlines for extracurricular activity enrollment	_____	_____
Other _____	_____	_____
Other _____	_____	_____
Other _____	_____	_____
Other _____	_____	_____
Other _____	_____	_____
Other _____	_____	_____
Other _____	_____	_____
Other _____	_____	_____
Other _____	_____	_____
Other _____	_____	_____

three: managing your home and property

Somewhere between perfection and chaos, every family needs to find *common ground*. Smooth functioning of the Home and Property department (not to mention a peaceful relationship) depends on it. Spelling out responsibilities—he cleans the kitchen and family room, she covers the bathroom and bedroom—without first negotiating specs for each room or task is a recipe for disaster.

Everyone has a different tolerance level for dirt and disorder. What qualifies as clean and tidy to one person may be filthy and disgusting to another. And often couples don't discover that they've married their housekeeping opposite until after they've set up house together.

Take Christina and Tim (not their real names), for example. Christina graduated with honors and was hired by a top accounting firm. She loves numbers and precision. Excel spreadsheets stoke her fire. One of her first assignments was to remedy sloppy bookkeeping practices that had evolved into serious problems for a key client. She worked diligently and finished the project ahead of schedule. The client was extremely pleased, and so was her boss. She was promoted after only six months on the job. But not everything in her life was rosy. You see, her penchant for putting details in order was putting her stomach out of order. When medical tests revealed an ulcer, Christina knew she needed to slow down and lighten up.

A few weeks after her promotion and diagnosis, Christina met Tim at a mutual friend's birthday party. He was the life of the party, sculpting crazy hats out of balloons and making everyone laugh.

Christina needed to laugh. She was having more fun than she'd had in months. At dinner she sat across the table from Tim and learned that he loved his job as a high school art teacher. He invited her to attend an art exhibit where the works of some of his students were on display. She accepted, and the day turned out to be fun for both of them—so they began to see each other regularly.

Christina admired Tim's passion for teaching and his love for kids. She enjoyed his humorous comments and spontaneous nature, and the way he loosened her up. Just what the doctor ordered.

Tim admired Christina's giftedness too. He was thrilled when she offered to help him with his tax return. It took a while, but he finally found most of the information she needed. He was amazed at her way with numbers. She even set up files for his receipts and important documents. And on top of this . . . she was beautiful!

As you've probably guessed, Tim and Christina married, and it wasn't long before their personal preferences and housekeeping differences fueled heated discussions. The very things that drew them to each other were now driving them crazy. His messy habits and unfinished creative projects coupled with her nagging and nitpicking standards laid the foundation for a wall of resentment between them. The more Christina tried to reform Tim, the more he resisted. She felt that if he really loved her, he would do things her way. The more Tim tried to get Christina to loosen up, the stiffer she became. He felt that if she really loved him, she would love him "as is." The wall between them grew higher and higher until finally it tumbled down and crushed their marriage.

warning: housekeeping opposites attract

What about you? Are you married to your housekeeping opposite?

Hands shot up when I asked that question at a women's retreat. "My husband's a slob . . . and I make Mr. Clean look remedial," one woman shouted from the back of the room.

As I told the group, differences aren't grounds for divorce— they're a chance to find common ground. Here's a good rule of thumb: *home should be clean enough to be healthy and dirty enough to be happy.*

Of course you say no to grunge. But who needs immaculate conditions if Mom or Dad has become the family nag in chief?

Remember, it's not an elected position. You appoint yourself. And if you're serious about creating a happy home, now's a good time to resign—*effective immediately*. A sparkling sink is just not that important.

To reduce conflict, however, you might consider working with your family to develop standard operating procedures (SOPs). These are simply established household routines that help make things run more smoothly. For instance, if you hate having to pile up the breakfast dishes on the counter each morning, you might determine to always empty the dishwasher before going to bed. You might decide to change the sheets on the first and fifteenth of every month or clean out your refrigerator the night before garbage pickup so you don't waste time deciding when to do regular chores like these. (For a worksheet your family can use to begin brainstorming SOPs for your household, see page 191 in chapter 9.)

SOPs help free up time and energy, and they will help your family stick to your priorities. They also give family members security because everyone knows what to expect. SOPs can be established for many tasks in all seven departments, including:

- meal planning
- kids' homework
- food shopping
- shopping for clothes
- cooking and preparing meals
- exercising
- cleaning up after meals
- running errands
- straightening up the house
- taking clothes to the cleaners
- vacuuming
- car maintenance

- making beds
- yard work
- doing laundry
- watering plants
- cleaning bathrooms
- pet care
- collecting and putting out trash
- recycling
- family paperwork— finances/bill paying
- school day mornings

In our family, housecleaning falls into the humorous fiction genre. At a recent family get-together, we listened and laughed as my parents reminisced about how back in the day—way back— a radio show character named Fibber McGee kept a closet the way hurricanes keep a shoreline. When the door opened on Fibber McGee's in-home storage unit, all of America heard a mountain of clutter clatter down and across the floor.

GOOD TO KNOW

Nearly half of moms blame household tasks for causing many arguments with their spouses, according to iRobot Corporation's "Balance at Home" survey.

I guess history repeats itself because, as I've confessed in other books, "domestically challenged" described me to a T when our family was young. Bill accused me of adding a mildew cycle to our washing machine. When I turned the boys' underwear pink, they insisted on doing their own laundry. (Remedial housekeeping has some benefits!)

Many days a vacuum cleaner couldn't do the job at our house. I needed a small bulldozer to clear a path through the clutter first. At times our bathroom qualified as a toxic waste site. And while I'm on the subject, let the record reflect that I disagree with whoever said, "Cleanliness is next to godliness." I don't know anyone who's had a religious experience scrubbing a shower stall. I sure haven't.

don't drown in your own clutter

But housekeeping standards are anything but funny to some people. I'm writing this paragraph on the plane, recalling vividly how last night after I spoke at an event, Katie walked up to me with tears in her eyes. She said some nights she just shut down when she walked into her home. Exhausted after teaching second graders all day, she felt helpless to tackle the chaos that surrounded her. She said that most every day, the first thing she saw when she walked in the door was a chair mounded with unfolded laundry. Then she'd walk into the kitchen, where the table and countertops were strewn with mail, kids' papers, receipts, coupons, and catalogs. Dishes were usually piled in the sink.

"I feel like I am slowly drowning in my own home," Katie said. "At school I can keep my desk, supply closet, and classroom neat and organized, but I can't seem to do the same at home." She said her husband and two sons didn't help out much, and she was about at her wit's end. She was desperate to know how to start getting her home and life back under control.

I asked Katie after the retreat to take the online Family Manager Assessment, which would reveal her priorities, stress points, and areas for change. Her answers would be used to create a personalized, sensible plan for getting her home back on track. Katie's assessment report revealed that the Family Manager departments in which she excelled were Family and Friends (relationships are important to her, and she's a gifted teacher) and Special Events

QUICK FIX

QUESTION: *My husband says he doesn't like to be told what to do, but he doesn't know what needs to be done around the house unless I tell him.*

ANSWER: A lot of men don't like to be told what to do, especially if it involves things they don't like to do or things about which they feel inept. Try making a list of 20 chores and asking him if he would pick 10. Asking goes a lot further than telling, and this way he can choose which ones he feels he can succeed at. Be sure to show appreciation for his efforts.

FROM THE HEART

Working together to make your house a home and devising a fair and efficient way to care for your home and belongings will save you a lot of stress—both now and in the years to come.

(she's energized by planning and throwing parties, celebrating holidays, and making occasions uniquely memorable). Not surprisingly, her most challenging department turned out to be Home and Property. She'd rather do most anything than laundry and housework. I can relate. (In fact, chapter 2 of *The Busy Mom's Guide to a Happy, Organized Home* is filled with ideas on clutter control, home organization, and cleaning shortcuts I've developed in my own quest to become more proficient in this department.)

Katie's plan started with a family meeting. Before things could significantly change, she needed to win over her husband and two sons, ages 7 and 11. I coached her on strategies for conducting a successful meeting and how to broach the subject of teamwork with her husband. (To read many of these tips, see chapter 9.)

Fast-forward: Katie was able to get buy-in from her family, and the first room they tackled was the kitchen. They set up "Control Central" at the kitchen desk. This would serve as their family's base of operation for scheduling and organizing mail, receipts, and other important papers. They decided to make a game out of clutter control by fining each other if belongings or papers were haphazardly placed on the kitchen table or countertops. The boys were excited about the potential to fine Mom or Dad for dropping their belongings too. After a trip to the office-supply store for a few organizing supplies, they all worked together to throw away or store the random items and paper clutter that had rendered their kitchen inefficient—and depressed Katie. That night they had dinner at their table for the first time in a long while.

At their family meeting they used a Who's Responsible for What? form (see page 58) to divide up household chores—including laundry, which the boys could fold in exchange for watching 30 minutes of TV after school.

The last time we spoke, Katie said they are still working on the strategies in their action plan, their home is getting a little more organized each week, and she's in a better mood at the end of the day—which, she said, may be the most important benefit of all.

pressure points and stress relief

We all carry stress from the outside world into our homes. A first grader who isn't picked until the last round for kickball has stressful feelings of rejection. When Dad's proposal is scrapped at the office, he may feel discouraged. Mom has a flat tire on the freeway in rush-hour traffic and quickly feels her anxiety mounting. Ideally, home is a place where we put away stress and recharge our batteries. While there is no such thing as a perfect home, there are some simple ways to reduce the stress level and make your home a more refreshing, enjoyable place for all.

First, you need to identify the recurring pressure points in your home. Some of the examples below may seem like little things. But when you confront them day after day, or when you're faced with a pile of them all at once, they can wear you down. Dealing with recurring stressors requires a lot of emotional energy.

Do you feel frustrated when you walk through your house and . . .

- your teenage daughter's empty soda can is on the end table—again?
- your third grader's science fair project is scattered all over the game table?
- there's cat hair in every corner and spiderwebs festooning the ceiling?
- the leaky faucet—going on three months—still drips?
- no one cleaned up the mud your dog tracked in from outside?
- you have to tell your son almost every day to get his size 12 feet off the coffee table?

SMART MOVE

One of our favorite household tools is a label maker. You can label shelves in your pantry, in closets, and in garage and storage areas where you keep tools, sports gear, games, and craft materials. Knowing where items belong reduces frustration because family members know where to find things and where to put things away. Labeling plastic storage bins also promotes household organization.

GOOD TO KNOW

Stress is the reaction we have to small irritations or big catastrophes. Over time stress can promote high blood pressure, a weakened immune system, heart disease, arthritis, and other ailments.

- your mother-in-law hints that you're a bad housekeeper because toys are scattered everywhere?
- you can't park one car in your two-car garage?

And what about your spouse and children?
Do they feel frustrated because . . .

- you nag them to do chores they didn't agree to do?
- they don't get a say about when and how chores should be done?
- they can't bring friends home because the place is too messy? Or too clean?
- they don't have any place they can call their own to work on hobbies or just be?
- they can't find the cleaner you told them to use in the kitchen?
- they don't know how to organize their things because they don't have the right supplies and no one's ever showed them how?
- they wish you would be more fun and quit worrying about dust?

QUICK FIX

QUESTION: *We've delegated chores to our children, but they simply won't cooperate. I usually end up doing the jobs myself because I don't want to start an argument.*

ANSWER: Never take no answer for an answer. And by all means, don't do the job yourself. If your kids watch TV, play video or electronic games, or spend personal time on the computer, relay this message to them: activities such as these are not God-given rights. They're privileges. And with privilege comes responsibility. When you help your kids connect those two big dots, you prepare them for the real world, where unfulfilled responsibilities mean no paycheck.

SMART MOVE

Managers of successful companies practice internal marketing. They educate team members, communicate with them in positive ways, and help them succeed at assigned jobs. The Family Manager's role is no different.

FROM THE HEART

Do not be your children's personal maid. Doing everything for them when you could teach them independence undermines both your life and theirs. Though you can do some things easier and faster, it's more important for them to develop life skills.

FROM THE HEART

Make sure your husband knows you're on his team. If you want him to lighten your load, make sure you are doing your part to ease the stresses in his life.

Every person and every family copes differently with dirt and clutter. No matter what your toleration level, working together to do away with some of the needless stress and creating a place that's user friendly for everyone can enhance your family's quality of life in significant ways. Whether you need to tweak a few areas or sense the need to totally revamp the way you run the Home and Property department, you may need to do some "internal marketing." And as in any business, the "continuing education" of team members is critical for success.

A series of family meetings could be one time to discuss these topics. But if you and your husband agree that a major change is needed, you might consider carving out a more lengthy time slot for a Family Manager workshop for your team—even if you and your spouse are the only ones on the team. Devoting this amount of time sends a powerful message that your family is changing directions on something important. At the same time, everyone in your family will come away feeling like they've been heard, and they will have a better understanding of how important they are to your family's team. Chapter 9 includes a plan to help you organize your own Family Manager workshop.

QUICK FIX

QUESTION: *Clutter has taken over our home. Our schedule is jammed, and we can't stop life to clear things out and get organized. Where can we start?*

ANSWER: Declutter a little at a time and make it fun. Conduct a clutter contest. Give each family member a plastic trash bag. Walk through your house and see how much clutter you can each collect in 15 minutes. The winner is the person with the most clutter in his or her bag when the time is up. Reward the winner. Do this a few days in a row, and you'll be amazed how much you can accomplish working together for just 15 minutes.

a man's point of view

managing home and property

Overseeing the Home and Property department is a bigger job than most of us guys realize. Sure, we know that a home has to be cleaned and belongings need to be maintained, but we often don't think about all this encompasses: the house, yard, furniture, accessories, decor, appliances, tools, electronic equipment, books, clothing, toys, and sports equipment, to name a few. We're talking about cleaning, storing, maintaining, organizing, redoing, and decorating—living rooms and workrooms and garages and cars and closets and basements and attics. We're talking about order and clutter and the stuff of daily living.

I have a friend who has the luxury of a full-time housekeeper, handyman, and groundskeeper, but for the rest of us the job of overseeing the acquisition, usage, storage, and maintenance of our homes and property can be more than a full-time job. Many of our belongings need some type of routine care and maintenance, and some need periodic repairs and improvements. How well we care for and maintain them has a lot to do with how much money we end up spending on those repairs and improvements.

We do ourselves and our wives a big favor by taking the time to understand all that needs to be done to care for our resources and then working as a team to make sure things get done. Managing this department takes a variety of tasks and skills, from the simplest, like picking up toys after toddlers; to the most repetitive, like doing the laundry; to those that draw on our creative and technical skills, like redecorating the living room or upgrading the family computer. And of course, managing Home and Property draws on planning, organization, and delegation skills, because no matter who you are, there are some jobs and tasks in this department we will want or need to delegate to others, either by hiring an expert or by relying on another family member's expertise.

TECH TIP

Use free online tools to help manage your home and property. PackAndFind.com allows you to inventory what you own and where it's stored. YourGarageOnline.com helps you keep up with your vehicles' routine maintenance and repairs.

SMART MOVE

Work together to create a network of friends and neighbors to trade skills and share household items. You might help your neighbors paint their kitchen; they help you install a tile backsplash.

HIGHLY RECOMMENDED

I encourage you to work with your wife and kids (if they're old enough) to come up with your family's definition of clean. I don't know what "normal" is for you, but chances are it's different from your spouse's. (To find out, I encourage you to complete the His Normal–Her Normal worksheet on page 52.) Personally, I have yet to figure out how Kathy immediately spots things left undone—who cares if a cabinet is open, the sofa throw isn't folded, or there's a spot or two on the carpet?—in a room I've cleaned just before guests arrive.

Even so, the apostle Peter said in 1 Peter 3 that husbands are to live with their wives in an understanding way. That means I need to take into consideration how God designed my wife. If she's weak in the Home and Property department but is a whiz at pulling off Special Events, I need to praise her for all she does to make celebrations so memorable and look for ways to work with her to shore up the Home and Property department. On the other hand, if I'm the one adding stress to her life by thoughtlessly dropping my belongings throughout the house—and then getting mad because I can't find them—I need to work on changing my ways. A sincere apology may be in order too.

See if you can work together to come up with definitions of *clean* and *organized* that you both can live with. When you give a little and she gives a little, you both live a lot better.

On pages 56–58 you'll find a room-by-room assessment and other worksheets to help you assess where you are, envision what you'd like to change, and craft an action plan to get there. Please don't take these pages lightly. Many people have said that these simple exercises saved their marriage.

create user-friendly rooms

When it comes to their home and property, most couples are concerned about keeping things clean, clutter free, and well maintained, but you can also make your home a more pleasant place by taking a larger view. No single element makes home a good place to be, but a number of things, working together, produce a pleasant environment.

All of us interpret our environment through our five senses. I use the five senses as a guide to help me create a "good place" for all of us. You might find it helpful, as Bill and I do, to ask yourselves some questions about what your family "senses" as they walk into your house:

Do you have rooms that seem dark?
Dark rooms can be depressing, as well as hard on your eyes if it's where you read or work on projects. You might need to replace existing overhead light fixtures with ones that give off more light, or place reading lamps next to seating.

Do rooms seem enclosed or light and airy?
Too much furniture and clutter in a room can make it visually shrink in size. Evaluate what's taking up space. Does it really need to be there?

Are there items and accessories—art, photos, mementos—in each room that bring to mind good memories?
I love to walk into our formal living room and remember how excited Bill and I were to find a wingback chair for thirty-five dollars at an estate sale one weekend when our kids were young. Though I could have bought a new chair with the money we've spent over the years on repairs and upholstery fabric, I keep it for the memory. Almost everything in our home has a story behind it— items we picked up on vacation and hauled back on the top of our car, gifts from family and friends, things we scrimped and saved for before purchasing.

Is the furniture in each room comfortable?
We once bought a sofa that was the right style, the right size, and the right color, but we didn't think about the fact that the fabric was scratchy and uncomfortable to exposed skin.

What does your home smell like?
Every home has a certain scent. Good smells in a home create an immediate sense of a pleasant environment. On the other hand, a

GOOD TO KNOW

The top three disorganized rooms in the house, in successive order, are the bedroom, garage, and home office/ den, reports the National Association of Professional Organizers.

HIS NORMAL—HER NORMAL

home and property

Think about the conflicts between you and your spouse that stem from the different ways your families managed your home and property when you were growing up. Discuss assumptions that you both brought into your marriage about "normal" ways to deal with the stuff in your life, as well as your definitions of clean and organized. Listen and learn from each other, then negotiate your way to the "new normal" for your relationship. (See examples below.)

His Normal	**Our New Normal**	**Her Normal**
I didn't get my own car until I was a junior in college. It meant a lot to me, and I took care of it and kept it immaculate. In my family, how well we took care of something showed how much we appreciated and valued it. I'm really bothered to see one of our cars look like a wreck inside.	We will try to keep both automobiles clean and well serviced. Since we realize that kids can make big messes, we'll put a trash can in the garage and try to clean trash out of the car daily. If Mom gets behind, Dad will help out (without complaining) by cleaning up the car every Saturday.	I was the oldest of five children, and my mom's car always had soggy cookies on the seats and cereal on the floor from my younger siblings. I was embarrassed when it was our turn to do the car pool, but now with kids of my own, I understand. Keeping a spotless car is just not that important.
His Normal	**Our New Normal**	**Her Normal**

home with bad odors can seem unwelcoming—even offensive. Leave your home for a while; then do a smell test when you walk back in.

Are we maximizing the potential of the rooms in our home?
If your answer is "No" or "We're not sure," I encourage you to grab a pen and a legal pad or a clipboard with paper to jot down notes and comments. Then walk around every room in your house and together answer these three questions:

1. What do we use this space for?
2. Is the current setup conducive to that use?
3. Are we satisfied with the use we currently make of the space?

As you evaluate your use of each space, keep the following in mind:

- If because of changing family circumstances, such as a new baby, you will need to convert a separate office or sewing room into a nursery, you may be forced to rethink the first question. What changes might you make to create room for these activities somewhere else?
- Consider how well the furniture, electronic equipment, and appliances in each room contribute to the way you'd like to use a room. For instance, if your family room is set up mostly for watching television but your family doesn't watch much TV, you might consider putting the set on a rolling cart that can be stashed in a closet, leaving room for a table for games, homework, or hobbies.
- Setting up or decorating rooms so they're conducive to their primary use involves several considerations. Is there enough light? space? Are the supplies you need in that room stored so they're accessible? Are the furnishings and decor in line with both your family's style and the way you use the room?
- Creating user-friendly rooms doesn't mean you have to go out and spend hundreds or thousands of dollars to drastically change each room in the house. Some small changes can make a big difference. Make this "house walk" an annual event to be sure you're getting the most out of your home.
- The Internet is full of great information and resources on home decorating. In addition to collecting online information

TECH TIP

If you are planning to decorate or just move some of your furniture to different spots in your home, pull up two chairs in front of a computer and download Sweet Home 3D software (sweet-home-3d. software.informer .com). You can create and analyze different options by setting the size and types of furniture you want to move around, add to, or remove from a room.

SMART MOVE

Decide as a couple how clean is clean enough; how fast is fast enough; and how much work, time, money, and energy to devote to each area of your home. Don't fall into the "Mother (or sister or best friend) knows best" trap or the "What will the neighbors think?" trap. Your standards are your standards, and they're the ones you should be striving to meet.

and bookmarking favorite Web site resources, keep a home journal—a notebook with one or more pages devoted to each room of your house. A simple five-subject notebook with dividers and folder pockets is ideal. Jot down problems and possible solutions. Look through magazines or catalogs for solution ideas. Clip them and put them in the notebook so when you're ready to make changes you'll have a variety of solutions to choose from. Keep paint chips and fabric swatches in the folder pockets. As you complete projects, note the salient details in your notebook.

10 Reasons You'll Never Get Organized and Stay That Way

1. Toddlers are the closest thing to perpetual-motion machines we'll ever see.
2. Pasta boils over and washing machine hoses burst.
3. The dog will escape and come home wearing the neighbor's garbage right before a Realtor and prospective buyer come to see your house.
4. Dropping everything to console a sad child is a lot more important than cleaning out the basement.
5. The best-laid plans are often led astray by sick children, a beautiful day that's better spent in the park, or any one of an almost infinite number of possibilities that can throw you off track.
6. The cat will hide in the back of the closet when it's time to go to the vet.
7. A fuse will blow right before your holiday party.
8. Sleep is more important than a perfectly organized linen closet.
9. Children are predictably unpredictable.
10. Life changes. Regularly.

the truth about clutter and cleaning

Getting your home clean and organized is an ongoing process, not an end product. Bathrooms, once clean, have a way of getting dirty. Dishes get left in the sink. Even so, the ACT worksheets will help you begin working together and more efficiently so the process is less onerous and your home is more enjoyable.

THE MOST IMPORTANT THINGS TO REMEMBER

1. Somewhere between perfection and chaos, every couple needs to find common ground about what makes home a good place to be for all.

2. Everyone has a different tolerance level for dirt and disorder. Spelling out responsibilities without first negotiating specs for each room or task is a recipe for disaster.

3. Working together to make your house a home and devising a fair and efficient way to care for your home and belongings will save you a whole lot of stress—both now and in the years to come.

4. Everyone who lives under the roof of a home should contribute to its upkeep. This is not the job of one or two people.

5. Don't assume that certain tasks are always the husband's or wife's responsibility. Let giftedness and time availability, not tradition, guide you as you share the load.

6. The more you accumulate, the more you have to clean and maintain—and the more time it takes to do it.

7. When your kids grow up and leave home, they won't remember if everything is perfect; they will remember if home was a good place to be and if Mom and Dad were fun people to be around.

8. If you have a choice between taking a family vacation and buying new furniture, go for the vacation. The furniture will end up in a garage sale one day; the memories of the trip will last forever.

9. While there is no such thing as a perfect home, working together to do away with some of the needless stress and creating a place that's user friendly for everyone can enhance your family's quality of life in big ways.

10. Creating a clean, organized home is an ongoing process, not an end product.

home and property department

Take a few minutes to think about the key causes of stress in the Home and Property department of your home. You and your spouse should use a different color pen or pencil to circle the number that best describes your individual stress level for each topic.

Key: 1=No Stress; 5=Very Stressful (0=Not Applicable)

General clutter/disorganization	0	1	2	3	4	5
Closets/drawers/storage spaces	0	1	2	3	4	5
Attic	0	1	2	3	4	5
Basement	0	1	2	3	4	5
Garage	0	1	2	3	4	5
Entry	0	1	2	3	4	5
Kitchen	0	1	2	3	4	5
Utility/mudroom	0	1	2	3	4	5
Dining room	0	1	2	3	4	5
Family room	0	1	2	3	4	5
Home office	0	1	2	3	4	5
Toy/playroom	0	1	2	3	4	5
Master bedroom	0	1	2	3	4	5
_____'s bedroom	0	1	2	3	4	5
_____'s bedroom	0	1	2	3	4	5
_____'s bedroom	0	1	2	3	4	5
_____'s bedroom	0	1	2	3	4	5
Guest bedroom	0	1	2	3	4	5
Bathroom 1	0	1	2	3	4	5
Bathroom 2	0	1	2	3	4	5
Bathroom 3	0	1	2	3	4	5
Bathroom 4	0	1	2	3	4	5
Thorough housecleaning	0	1	2	3	4	5
Laundry	0	1	2	3	4	5
Toys/sports gear	0	1	2	3	4	5
Mail/paper clutter	0	1	2	3	4	5
Hobby supplies/equipment	0	1	2	3	4	5
Other _____	0	1	2	3	4	5
Other _____	0	1	2	3	4	5
Other _____	0	1	2	3	4	5
Other _____	0	1	2	3	4	5
Other _____	0	1	2	3	4	5

home and property department

Your Priorities

Look again at the items in the previous chart that you ranked as a 4 or a 5. Then you and your spouse should read the "I want" statements below and place a check in the box next to the ones that best describe your priorities for managing the Home and Property department. Circle two or three that you each deem most important.

I want ...

his	hers	
❑	❑	to declutter our home and get organized.
❑	❑	to catch up and keep up with housework.
❑	❑	to catch up and keep up with laundry.
❑	❑	to conquer paper clutter and create a system for filing important papers.
❑	❑	to work as a family team on household chores.
❑	❑	to remember that people are more important than a picture-perfect home.
❑	❑	to create a comfortable and welcoming environment.
❑	❑	to decorate and update areas of our home.
❑	❑	to maximize the storage spaces in our home.
❑	❑	to make some of the rooms in our home more user friendly.
❑	❑	to maintain our home and care for our belongings so what we own lasts longer.
❑	❑	to make our home a safer place.
❑	❑	_____
❑	❑	_____
❑	❑	_____
❑	❑	_____

Your Goal

Consider your individual and shared priorities, then write an overall goal that reflects your desires for the Home and Property department. For this purpose, think of a goal as a broad, general, timeless statement that describes your overall aim for this department. Sometimes it is helpful to begin by identifying the key words that you'd use to describe this department when it runs well. Here's an example:

> **Key Words:** *clean, attractive, well-maintained, comfortable haven, enjoy, welcoming*
>
> **Goal:** *To care for our home and belongings in such a way that we can enjoy them as much as possible and they will last as long as possible; to decorate our home attractively and keep it reasonably clean so our family and friends enjoy being there.*

Key Words: _____

_____

Goal: _____

_____

home and property department

Using this worksheet, divide up responsibilities for the Home and Property department.

Who's Responsible for What?

Responsibilities	Who does it now?	Who else could do it?
Daily cleaning/clutter pickup	_____	_____
Clean the kitchen	_____	_____
Clean the bathrooms	_____	_____
Clean the family room	_____	_____
Sweep/mop/wax floors	_____	_____
Dust	_____	_____
Vacuum	_____	_____
Deep cleaning	_____	_____
Organize closets and drawers	_____	_____
Organize basement	_____	_____
Water plants	_____	_____
Clean carpets	_____	_____
Wash windows	_____	_____
Communicate with housekeeper or cleaning service	_____	_____
Make beds	_____	_____
Change sheets	_____	_____
Do laundry	_____	_____
Take clothes to dry cleaner	_____	_____
Mend clothes	_____	_____
Shop for clothes and other items	_____	_____
Shop for household items	_____	_____
Decorate/acquire furnishings	_____	_____
Collect and take out trash	_____	_____
Recycle	_____	_____
Do household repairs and maintenance	_____	_____
Contact repair services	_____	_____
Maintain yard/landscaping	_____	_____
Maintain yard/pool/outdoor equipment	_____	_____
Maintain outdoor furniture	_____	_____
Organize garage	_____	_____
Maintain vehicles	_____	_____
Clean vehicles	_____	_____
Other _____	_____	_____
Other _____	_____	_____
Other _____	_____	_____
Other _____	_____	_____
Other _____	_____	_____

four: managing menus and meals

All of us meet our Family Manager duties with different levels of skill and varying degrees of confidence. Some women (though not this one) manage family finances on Excel spreadsheets with neat categories and columns that balance. Others are one-woman cleaning machines. Caring for home and property is where they shine. Still others can throw open the refrigerator door . . . and reframe leftovers to create a meal fit for royalty. The Food department just comes naturally to this last group.

No Family Manager excels at every department, and every Family Manager oversees one or more departments that need at least some bolstering.

If the Food department is a challenge for you, as it is for me, you'll want to bookmark this section and pull up a chair for your husband. Because, as I'm sure you're aware, managing menus and meals efficiently—deciding what's for dinner; shopping for groceries; considering nutrition, family member preferences, and the rising cost of food—is a very important, very daily responsibility. Two heads and four hands are better than one departmentally challenged person—on a number of levels.

Author Malcolm Gladwell, who wrote *The Tipping Point*, describes the difference between a puzzle and a mystery. A puzzle, he says, is solved with information. A mystery, no matter how much information is amassed, remains a mystery; more information tends only to cloud it further. I couldn't have put that thought into words when I was new at my Family Manager role, but the more cookbooks I read and recipes I tried, the more I believed cooking was in the realm of mystery.

GOOD TO KNOW

Preparing a home-cooked meal requires an average of 34 minutes of hands-on time, according to UCLA's Sloan Center on Everyday Lives of Families.

TECH TIP

If you are wondering what's for dinner, allrecipes.com lets you choose recipes based on main ingredients, what you have on hand, and how much time you have for food prep. There's also a free iPhone app: AllRecipes.com Dinner Spinner.

culinary teamwork

One night after ruining another dinner, I began ravishing the newspaper for restaurant coupons. I told Bill we'd have to either eat out for the rest of our lives or hire a cook. With no apparent forethought, Bill said, "Love, I used to sit on a stool in the kitchen after school and watch my mother cook . . . and learned quite a bit in the process. Why don't I start doing some of the cooking?"

The mystery is my husband. He has a way of magically turning the mountains I've created back into molehills.

From that moment on, we began operating this department as a team. Once a month we have a cooking day. We decide what we're going to cook, then one of us will go to the grocery store, wholesale club, and/or farmers market and gather all the ingredients. I place everything out on the counter along with the recipe books, pots and pans, and utensils we'll need. I give Bill his apron, put on some music, and as the sous-chef, wait for him to tell me what he wants me to do. In one big pot we might stew chicken breasts for making chicken enchiladas, chicken spaghetti, chicken divan, and chicken noodle soup. In another big pot we might brown lean ground beef or ground turkey for chili and meatballs. We put six or eight meals in the freezer. Then we clean up together.

QUICK FIX

QUESTION: *I'm going back to work. What's a simple way my husband and I can divide dinner responsibilities?*

ANSWER: Try alternating nights: he cooks on Mondays and Wednesdays; you cook on Tuesdays and Thursdays. Grill out one weekend night, and have "planned-overs" to fill in the gaps. (Whenever possible, double or triple a recipe and freeze the leftovers for another night. Leftovers from one night's roast chicken can be turned into stir-fry, tacos, or sandwiches another night.)

So whether you regularly "kick it up a notch," à la Emeril, or open jars and boil pasta, working together makes this potentially overwhelming task infinitely doable.

Not only do we have all those meals prepared ahead of time, but we've spent an afternoon together. While we're chopping, sautéing, simmering, and roasting, we talk about current events, vacation dreams, the kids, and a number of other topics we might not have time to cover as we hurry through our usual schedules. Bill enjoys doing something with me, and I don't have to cook. It's a win-win solution.

Teamwork has solved many of my kitchen challenges. This may sound small and obvious, but I felt indescribably free when I decided it doesn't make me less of a woman, mother, or Family Manager to allow someone else—often my husband, who is infinitely more talented and comfortable in the kitchen than I am—to cook sometimes. (I should mention that our boys thought about hiring a marching band to celebrate when their father took over more of the cooking.) Today the young women who married our older two boys appreciate the fact that their men know their way around a kitchen.

a man's point of view

managing menus and meals

When you were growing up, who did the cooking, grocery shopping, and kitchen cleanup in your home? At my house, food just appeared. I knew that grocery shopping and cooking were involved, but I never thought much about the process or how much my mom did to make sure our family had not only good food but nutritious food.

I find that a lot of men don't think about food until they're hungry. That was my case, and because my mother did virtually all the work in this department, "normal" to me was the wife taking on the food preparation. Not that I wasn't willing to help. But I had no appreciation for what it took to plan, prepare, and provide 1,095 meals per year—not counting snacks, parties, and holiday celebrations.

What about in your home? Who decides what you'll eat? Who buys it and prepares it? On what schedule? Who decides where you eat and with whom and what goes on at mealtimes? Who cleans up? Who organizes the

GOOD TO KNOW

Thirty-four percent of Americans say they enjoy cooking "a great deal," and there is no gender bias. The Pew Center found that 32 percent of men and 35 percent of women say they enjoy cooking.

SMART MOVE

Many men say they get tired of hearing about "how it should be done" or that "this is *my* territory." So they give up and don't do anything. Welcome teamwork and don't overcritique. You'll get a lot more cooperation.

GOOD TO KNOW

Each year, the average-sized household in America spends about $3,500 per year on groceries and nearly $2,700 eating out, according to the U.S. Department of Labor.

kitchen and keeps it sanitary? Make no mistake. This is an important department of family management.

Managing the Menus and Meals department is about more than just filling hungry bellies. It's also about nutrition and fostering good health. Growing up in Texas, I acquired a taste for Southern foods such as chicken-fried steak with cream gravy. I was like Will Rogers in that I never met a fried food I didn't like. As a teenager, my criterion for determining good food was: does it taste good?

Fortunately, I married a woman who made the obvious connection between good health and good nutrition— and who helped me rework my definition of good food. Though I didn't always appreciate her opinions at first, through the years I learned that just as air and water quality are critical to health, so is a proper diet.

But there's even more at stake than a family's physical health. Shared meals are the great learning center of family life. There's something about sitting down and eating together, especially when everybody has had a hand—no matter how small—in getting the meal on the table, that brings closeness. I've learned that dinnertime is about a lot more than the food, because food shapes our families in ways we don't often think about. How we talk about food, how we act around it (good manners), as well as what we serve and when and under what circumstances we eat, say a lot about our family and give our children attitudes for life. Some simple questions will go a long way toward using mealtime to strengthen family bonds. Ask yourself:

How can I encourage my children and my wife as we start our day together over breakfast?
What topics are we going to talk about at the dinner table?
What family issues do we need to discuss together?
What can I relate to my family about my day so they'll understand some of what's going on in my work world, and how can I learn about and show concern for the goings-on of their day?

Obviously, I'm assuming that families should eat together—a critical component of family culture. Deciding with your spouse to eat a certain number of meals together as a family each week is one of the most important decisions you can make. Eating together provides an unparalleled opportunity for family discussion and the inculcation of values. Encourage conversation by banning TV and phone calls during dinner.

Like the rest of home operations, the Menus and Meals department works best when it's a team effort. Some men and women love to cook. Others don't. Management of menus and meals is not automatically more one spouse's job than the other's. Once again, this department is best managed after assessing each person's giftedness and time availability.

 HIGHLY RECOMMENDED

Sometime soon, sit down with your wife and talk about this department together. You might begin by completing the His Normal–Her Normal worksheet on page 64. Here are some questions to continue your discussion:

What are all the activities that need to take place for this department to run well?
What nutritional standards do we want as a family?
When will we eat and not eat?
Where will we eat and not eat?
What do we want mealtimes to be like?
How will we handle food likes and dislikes, and picky eaters?
How will we decide what to eat?
Who will do each job in the department?

GOOD TO KNOW

The more often families eat together, the less likely kids are to smoke, drink, do drugs, become depressed, develop eating disorders, and consider suicide. These children are also more likely to do well in school, delay having sex, eat vegetables, learn new vocabulary words, and have good table manners. "If it were just about food, we would squirt it into their mouths with a tube," notes Robin Fox, an anthropologist at Rutgers University. "A meal is about civilizing children. It's about teaching them to be a member of their culture."

a case for family dinnertime

Sometimes you just don't realize how bad a habit is until, when you're firmly entrenched in it, you suddenly become aware of unwanted and even dangerous side effects. Once you're aware of the potential dangers, you're motivated to change.

HIS NORMAL—HER NORMAL

menus and meals

Consider the conflicts between you and your spouse that stem from the different ways your families managed food and meals when you were growing up. Discuss assumptions that you each brought into your marriage about the "normal" ways families shop for groceries, prepare meals, and keep the kitchen running efficiently. Listen and learn from each other; then negotiate your way to the "new normal" for your relationship. (See examples below.)

His Normal	**Our New Normal**	**Her Normal**
Family meals were a big deal at our house. Maybe too big, considering we were all a little overweight. I want to eat healthier, but I think that meals are important and that we should put some effort into what we eat.	We will plan ahead so that we can make mealtimes a priority. And we will plan our menus and grocery shopping to be sure that what we serve is healthy and nutritious.	Both of my parents worked and shared the load. When I was old enough, I helped by doing the grocery shopping. We got something satisfying on the table, but food was really never a very important part of our life.
His Normal	**Our New Normal**	**Her Normal**

For example, when I learned I had breast cancer, I began researching ways to improve my health—solutions beyond prescriptions and radiation. In the process, I learned that certain foods are good to keep your body healthy and to help fight cancer. And I discovered that certain foods can encourage cancer growth.

Once I was armed with this information, why wouldn't I want to heed the advice? It is my responsibility to take care of myself as much as I can, to take control of what I can actually control. To do otherwise—to ignore the facts—would not be wise and could even be potentially dangerous.

Now let me ask you a question. If you learned that by making just one change you could increase the chances of your children getting good grades and decrease the chances that your children would use drugs and alcohol, would you implement that change? What if you learned that your current habits were getting in the way of providing the most nurturing environment for your family?

Many families say their schedules are so complex that it's just too hard to get everyone around the table for dinner at the same time. If this is true at your home, may I remind you of a few facts—in hopes that you will do whatever it takes to eat together at least a few nights each week.

- According to the Society for Research in Child Development, sharing a meal regularly can boost children's health and well-being, reducing the likelihood that they will become obese or use drugs, and increase the chances that they'll do well in school.
- The same group found that teens who eat five or more meals a week with their families are less likely to smoke cigarettes or marijuana and to abuse alcohol.
- A 2008 study from the University of Minnesota Medical School showed that adolescent girls who ate frequent meals with their families were half as likely to smoke, drink, and use marijuana as their peers.
- The National Center on Addiction and Substance Abuse (CASA) at Columbia University found that parents who eat with their children at least five times a week report having a better relationship with their children.
- CASA also found that teens who eat dinner with their families are more likely to receive A's and B's than teens

SMART MOVE

Consumer Reports studies show shoppers consistently save money buying food in bulk at warehouse stores like Costco and Sam's Club. However, a bulk-sized box of cereal isn't a good buy if half of it goes stale and uneaten. Brainstorm as a family and make a list of long-lasting bulk staples that make sense for your family to buy.

GOOD TO KNOW

Family dinner gets better with practice, according to the National Center on Addiction and Substance Abuse at Columbia University. The less often a family eats together, the worse the experience is likely to be, the less healthy the food, and the more meager the talk.

who do not. Preschoolers who eat dinner together with their families have better language skills because they hear adult conversation around the table.

Most family meals last, on average, 18 to 20 minutes. It's incredibly empowering to realize that in 20 short minutes every day, you can help set your children and your family on the right path—just by joining together toward the end of the day to share a meal.

While eating dinner together as a family doesn't guarantee that your child will make the honor roll or never smoke, the data shows that your chances are better if you regularly eat dinner together as a family. Now that you're armed with the facts, why would you take the risk of not eating together?

Of course, if you're not already in the habit of eating together, you may feel daunted by the need to pull everyone back to the table at the same time. If so, try some of these techniques to reinstate and enjoy family dinnertime at your home:

1. *Keep it simple.* Don't worry if you don't have time to make the meal from scratch. The act of eating together alone has huge benefits. Even takeout eaten together counts as a family meal.
2. *Predetermine and post menus.* You can prevent frustration over what to fix for dinner by planning your menus ahead.
3. *Assign everyone a meal-related job.* Working on meals with other family members teaches kids responsibility and important life skills.
4. *Make attendance nonoptional.* Mom and Dad decide which nights your family will eat together each week. Agree that this is a priority, even if your kids protest. If you have teenagers, you might consider allowing them to invite a friend for dinner every now and then.
5. *Disconnect from the world and connect with your family.* Turn off the TV and ban phone calls, texting, and reading e-mail during dinner.
6. *Keep the conversation positive and relaxed.* Invite family members to share funny or uplifting stories about what happened in their day. Ban critical words and arguing. Avoid disciplinary discussions that could be handled another time. Dinner is not the time to talk about chores or problems at school.

7. *Set the example.* Model good table manners for your children. Proper etiquette will take your kids far in life. Require proper attire—shirts, no hats—for the dinner table. And Mom and Dad: eat your vegetables if you want your kids to eat theirs.

8. *Start and finish together.* Everyone who is at home should be seated at the beginning of the meal. Say a prayer of thanksgiving before eating. Get into the habit of having family members remain at the table until everyone is excused.

9. *Just do it.* If your schedule will simply not allow you to eat dinner together every night, aim for at least two or three nights per week. Try to eat breakfast together and lunch on weekends.

nutrition 101

Deciding to make family dinnertime a priority can make a vital difference in your kids' well-being. Of course, good nutrition also contributes to their overall health. As you plan meals, keep in mind these recommendations from the U.S. Department of Agriculture:

1. *Make half your grains whole.* Choose whole-grain foods, such as whole-wheat bread, oatmeal, brown rice, and lowfat popcorn, more often.

2. *Vary your veggies.* Go dark green and orange with your vegetables—eat spinach, broccoli, carrots, and sweet potatoes.

3. *Focus on fruits.* Eat them at meals, and at snack time, too. Choose fresh, frozen, canned, or dried, and go easy on the fruit juice.

4. *Get your calcium-rich foods.* To build strong bones serve lowfat and fat-free milk and other milk products several times a day.

5. *Go lean with protein.* Eat lean or lowfat meat, chicken, turkey, and fish. Also, change your tune with more dry beans and peas. Add chick peas, nuts, or seeds to a salad; pinto beans to a burrito; or kidney beans to soup.

6. *Change your oil.* We all need oil. Get yours from fish, nuts, and liquid oils such as corn, soybean, canola, and olive oil.

7. *Don't sugarcoat it.* Choose foods and beverages that do not have sugar and caloric sweeteners as one of the first ingredients. Added sugars contribute calories with few, if any, nutrients.[4]

CAUTION!

Don't scrimp on nutrition when you save on food. One ironic consequence of economic stress tends to be obesity, as consumers substitute cheaper foods that can fill them up. Researchers at the University of Washington determined that junk food costs an average of $1.76 per 1,000 calories, while unprocessed foods run $18.16 per 1,000 calories.

FROM THE HEART

When I was growing up in the South, we always had a container of pimento cheese in the refrigerator. After school, I often headed to the kitchen to make a pimento cheese sandwich. Although we've changed Mom's recipe to accommodate our waistlines and desire to eat healthier, a pimento cheese sandwich on whole-grain bread is a favorite comfort food that takes me back to sultry Memphis afternoons in our comfy kitchen. What comfort-food memories will your kids remember when they're grown?

QUICK FIX

QUESTION: *I've been stocking up on more healthy foods, like fruits, vegetables, and yogurt, because my spouse and I want us—and our kids—to eat better. While we're eating better at mealtimes, snacks are a different story. What can I do to encourage our kids to choose fresh fruit or crackers over cookies when they grab a snack?*

ANSWER: The key to getting your family to choose healthy treats like grapes, apples, and veggies and dips is to make them easily accessible. If you buy a bag of grapes and stick it in the produce bin, chances are it will stay there. After a long day at school or work, few people will take the time to dig the grapes out and wash them. However, if you wash and dry the grapes when you get home from the store and place them in a see-through container in the front of your refrigerator, your family is more likely to grab a handful for a quick snack.

Just as important as making healthy snacks very visible is keeping tasty but less nutritious snacks out of sight. If searching through the pantry for the bag of chocolate chip cookies takes too long, your family is more likely to reach for the microwave popcorn or whole-wheat crackers that are in plain sight.

going to extremes can backfire

As I mentioned in chapter 2, I've found that striving for balance doesn't work for all aspects of family management, but the Food department is one place where thinking in terms of balance is helpful. When it comes to managing the Food department, the person who oversees menus, meals, snacks, and grocery shopping—whether it's Mom, Dad, or both—has to find the balance between what's healthy, what's appetizing, what's affordable, and what's available—often ASAP. Sometimes all those things work together: no complaining and no guilt. Those are the good times . . . but for many Family Managers, they're few and far between.

Depending on how much guilt we're feeling and how much

we want to appease complaints, it's easy to overreact and go to extremes. At least I did.

When our oldest son was in first grade, I went on a serious nutrition binge and banned all foods with refined sugar or flour from our home. I drove to the country to buy honey, stocked up on undefiled grains from the health-food store, and baked homemade bread and various kinds of cookies (which we could have used for doorstops).

Every morning, with self-righteous zeal, I packed a healthy lunch for John: a sandwich built from the spoils of my health-food acquisitions and a few stone-ground wheat cookies. I turned up my nose at less conscientious mothers who put chips and sweets in their children's lunches. *How irresponsible!* I thought smugly.

When it came time for his parent-teacher conference, the teacher assured me that John was doing well in school. But she questioned my attitude toward nutrition. "Did you know, Mrs. Peel, that your son eats only chips and sweets for lunch most every day?" It seems that the other children felt sorry for John, so they took turns donating their extras to him. My nutritional binge ended—suddenly.

Here's the point: certainly you want to encourage your kids to eat healthy foods. But you'd best have some kid-friendly food on hand too if you want your kids and their friends hanging out at your house—especially when they're teenagers. I sure liked them being at our home, although this increased our grocery bill. (We nicknamed a couple of their friends Raiders of the Lost Fork). It was worth it to know whom our boys were spending time with and what they were doing.

preparation preempts problems

I've learned through trial and a lot of error that when you get the Food department under control, you preempt potential problems in other departments as well. You save time by eliminating last-minute trips to the store. You save money by cutting back on fast food because you have fast-fix options available.

When menus are planned in advance and your kitchen is stocked with all the food and ingredients you need, everyone tends to feel calmer and a sense of order pervades. Mornings are much calmer because you have breakfast foods on hand. When you forget to put chicken in the Crock-Pot and soccer practice runs late the same afternoon, you shift seamlessly to plan B because you have planned ahead for days like this. When your husband calls home on the

SMART MOVE

Freeze leftover Halloween candy. One mom I know takes some from each of her kids' Halloween bags and stores it in the freezer. Then, before heading to the community pool in the summer, she tosses a few frozen candy bars into the pool bag. They stay cold, she avoids spending money at the snack bar, and the kids get a kick out of eating Halloween candy in the summertime.

Meal Planning

Get the whole family involved in menu planning. Have everybody suggest his or her favorite foods, what each person would like to eat that you haven't fixed for a while, and maybe something you've never served but a child enjoyed at a friend's house. You can organize the brainstorming list as you go by meal (breakfast, lunch, dinner) or by category (fruit, vegetable, etc.). Or you can simply list everything and organize the foods into reasonable menus later.

Favorite Dishes

Meats	Vegetables	Fruits	Salads	Breads	Snacks	Desserts

Meal/Menu Ideas

Breakfasts	Lunches	Dinners

spur of the moment to tell you that he's bringing his boss by in 20 minutes, you simply shift into emergency guest-plan mode and pull out the hors d'oeuvres—the ones that you keep hidden from your kids for such a time as this.

And being prepared will get you in and out of the kitchen faster, which is a big benefit for those of us who dislike spending time in front of the stove.

spending less on food

Last-minute trips to the store or take-out place are neither time- nor cost-efficient. Cutting back on them will save you money. You can reduce your food budget in several other ways as well. A few pennies here, a dollar there—it all adds up. Most likely your family, like ours, has room to improve and save in the grocery store aisles.

Bill and I split grocery-shopping duties, and our strategy is pretty simple: we decide what we're going to eat and stick to a list. I like to shop on Tuesday mornings. A few years back I interviewed a grocery executive and learned that fewer people shop on Tuesdays (think: shorter lines) and the food is usually fresher. Shelves get restocked with fresh goods on Mondays after weekend plundering.

Though we're constantly looking for ways to cut food costs, we've never been serious coupon clippers—until recently, that is. That's when I met Ashley Nuzzo at a women's retreat where I was the speaker. After having her first child, Ashley wanted to leave her teaching job and stay home with her daughter. In order for her family to get by on one income, Ashley began treating saving money like a job—researching Web sites, reading blogs, printing online coupons, scouring the newspaper for discounts. *U.S. News & World Report* reported that she saves up to $1,500 a month! (If you want to find out how she does it—and how you can save big too— visit Ashley's Web site, http://www.frugalcouponliving.com.)

I asked Bill to create a custom-size bulletin board for one wall in our laundry room where our family could post coupons. This works well for us because the coupons are easy to see and grab when we're going to the store.

make couponing a family affair

- Kids can cut out and sort coupons while sitting in front of the TV.

GOOD TO KNOW

According to a 2009 National Restaurant Association report, 76 percent of adults polled said they are trying to eat healthier now at restaurants than they did two years ago.

Weekly Meal Planner

MENU		NOTES
Monday		
Tuesday		
Wednesday		
Thursday		
Friday		
Saturday		
Sunday		

- Circle or highlight expiration dates with two different colors for easy sorting. Use one color to highlight those with a short life span (within six weeks) and another color for those that give you a year or more to use them.
- A lot of people say storing coupons in labeled envelopes, an accordion file, or a coupon organizer works well. Or you might want to try our bulletin board idea. Your kids can make labels to designate categories, such as dairy, meat, baking supplies, cleaning products, and snacks, which can be placed across the top of the board. They can also help keep the board current by finding and tossing outdated coupons.

more ways to save at the grocery store

- Select items from the top and bottom shelves. More expensive merchandise is usually placed at eye level.
- Try less-expensive store brands. Many are made by well-known national brands, and they offer the same quality as the more expensive brands.
- Save about a dollar a pound on fresh produce by buying bagged rather than loose fruit and vegetables (such as onions, potatoes, apples, and oranges). No two bags weigh exactly the same, so use the produce scale to weigh a few bags before you choose one. You could get a few apples for free.
- Buy canned fruits and vegetables in smaller pieces. For example, pineapple chunks and diced tomatoes typically cost less than pineapple rings and whole tomatoes.
- Buy a beef or pork tenderloin and cut it into fillets and stew meat yourself. You'll save 25 to 30 percent over the cost of precut fillets or cubes.
- Expect about 45 percent waste if you discard the skin on chicken breasts. Boneless and skinless breasts may be a better buy.
- Don't let marketing phrases fool you. "New and improved" might mean only a new color or formula. Before you buy a product labeled "10% more free," compare it to other packages of the same product to be sure it's really economical.
- Be cautious of companion foods displayed together. The chips may be discounted, but the salsa could be premium priced.

GOOD TO KNOW

According to a 2009 *Consumer Reports* study, 35 percent of Americans rarely, if ever, use coupons. If you aren't clipping coupons for items you buy regularly, you're missing out on a tremendous opportunity to cut costs—about one dollar per item, on average.

SMART MOVE

One mom told me that on evenings when the family schedule is jammed, she orders takeout from a Thai restaurant at lunchtime to reheat for dinner. This saves her sanity, time, and money (since most restaurants charge lower prices at lunch than at dinner).

saving on food in your own backyard

Consider planting a garden—even if your thumb, like mine, is not the greenest one out there. The first summer I tried gardening, many plants died under my oversight. But the next summer I got the hang of it, and the zucchini multiplied like rabbits. Relishing my victory, I zealously stuffed zucchini, steamed zucchini, stir-fried zucchini, and baked zucchini bread and muffins. Finally, my family begged: no more zucchini! (That summer I learned that variety and moderation are important aspects of gardening.)

how dinnertime almost destroyed a marriage

When Bill and I met Phil and Courtney, they had been married for seven years and were the parents of three-year-old twin daughters. The couple had experienced the normal ups and downs of marriage, but then a local plant closed down, Phil lost his job, and things changed. He and a coworker saw the market niche that the plant closing left in the city, so they decided to start a new business to meet the need. Six months into the new venture, Courtney was not happy. It wasn't so much the financial risk of a start-up company but the fact that she never knew when Phil was coming home at night—which made her feel very unimportant. On the other hand, Phil felt unappreciated for what he was doing for their family. He was working hard to get the business off the ground and make enough to pay the bills.

Courtney had learned her view of "normal" in a home where her father had a steady job and came home every afternoon at 5:30. They ate dinner at 6:00 and enjoyed quiet evenings as a family until bedtime. She expected Phil to do the same. Of course, that rarely happened. At first she made him a plate and reheated it when he would drag in at 7:00 or later. But she grew tired of his tardiness and put down her foot: if he wasn't home by 6:00, he could take care of himself.

Phil grew up in an entrepreneurial family, so he learned that normal means working hard and doing what it takes to succeed—which in this season of life meant getting a new business up and running. He could settle into a better, more family-friendly routine later. He felt that Courtney was being incredibly unfair and unrealistic. He started work at 5:30 every morning and was simply putting in the hours that a start-up company demanded. His business partner didn't have children and would routinely work until 8:00 or later, so Phil felt unspoken pressure to match his partner's hours. He grew frustrated over Courtney's inability to understand that he couldn't just drop everything and follow her arbitrary dinner schedule.

Their relationship grew worse, and by the time the couple was sitting in our living room talking to Bill and me, they were one step away from divorce. After listening to both sides of the story, we asked them to answer two questions before we visited again.

1. *What goal does your spouse seem to be blocking?* Courtney said that she wanted to have a strong family life and that she wanted Phil to be more involved in their girls' lives. Phil said he wanted to make enough money so that Courtney could stay home with the girls.
2. *What would you be willing to do to move toward your spouse's goal?* Courtney said she would be willing to move dinner to a later time and feed the girls a healthy snack earlier, if need be. She also suggested that she and the girls could take dinner to the office sometimes when Phil couldn't get home to dinner. She would take a blanket, and they could have a picnic dinner on the floor. He appreciated her idea.

    Phil committed to being home for dinner by 6:30 at least two nights during the week. He said he would call home and let Courtney know his schedule each afternoon. He also promised to talk to his partner about his need to get home earlier unless he had to deal immediately with a crisis.

These simple steps the couple agreed to take ended up saving their marriage. Today, 20 years later, one of their daughters is in graduate school and the other is married and expecting a baby. Phil and Courtney teach the young couples' Sunday school class at their church. Willingness to make small changes can indeed make a big difference in a family.

To develop a good strategy for managing the food and meals at your home, work through the ACT process as a couple. Even if you're the gifted cook in the family and your spouse is culinarily challenged, you can help him master a few simple dishes; he can grill out on the weekends and clean up the kitchen. No one needs to be a gourmet cook to adequately feed and nourish a family.

FROM THE HEART

I once read that Samuel Johnson felt if you didn't dine well, the rest of your life was suspect. Whether you are eating at the kitchen table, in the dining room, or at a restaurant, some of your family's most treasured moments can occur when you come together to eat and enjoy each other's undivided attention.

THE MOST IMPORTANT THINGS TO REMEMBER

1. Shared meals are the great learning center of family life. There's something about sitting down and eating together, especially when everybody has had a hand, no matter how small, in getting the meal on the table, that brings closeness.

2. Like the other home operations, the Food department works best when it's a team effort. Food and teamwork go hand in hand, perhaps more naturally than any other area of family management. Eating and cooking together builds bonds.

3. Managing food and meals as a team and including children in age-appropriate ways teaches them invaluable life skills.

4. Managing menus and meals efficiently preempts potential problems in other departments by saving your family time, money, and aggravation.

5. When meals are planned in advance, with all the food and ingredients on hand, everyone tends to relax and feel calmer.

6. Your family eats 1,095 meals per year—snacks and parties not included—which means this is not a job for one person. Working as a couple to develop a good strategy for managing the Food department is a worthwhile endeavor.

7. What a family eats and drinks greatly influences the health of each member.

8. It is not necessary to have a gourmet cook in the house to adequately feed and nourish a family.

9. There is more to eating than good food. The ambience—where and how the table is set or how the picnic is organized—can make meals more pleasant and define family culture.

10. Reclaim the family dinner hour. Decide to eat together certain nights each week—and then don't let anything disrupt those plans.

menus and meals department

Take a few minutes to think about the key causes of stress in the Menus and Meals department of your home. You and your spouse should use a different color pen or pencil to circle the number that best describes your individual stress level for each topic.

Key: 1=No Stress; 5=Very Stressful (0=Not Applicable)

Meal planning	0	1	2	3	4	5
Grocery shopping	0	1	2	3	4	5
Pantry organization	0	1	2	3	4	5
Refrigerator/freezer organization	0	1	2	3	4	5
Using coupons	0	1	2	3	4	5
Breakfast preparation	0	1	2	3	4	5
Lunch preparation	0	1	2	3	4	5
Dinner preparation	0	1	2	3	4	5
Dinnertime experience	0	1	2	3	4	5
General kitchen cleaning	0	1	2	3	4	5
Post-meal cleanup	0	1	2	3	4	5
Kitchen countertops	0	1	2	3	4	5
Kitchen storage space	0	1	2	3	4	5
Kitchen functionality	0	1	2	3	4	5
Entertaining/hospitality	0	1	2	3	4	5
Other _____	0	1	2	3	4	5
Other _____	0	1	2	3	4	5
Other _____	0	1	2	3	4	5
Other _____	0	1	2	3	4	5
Other _____	0	1	2	3	4	5
Other _____	0	1	2	3	4	5
Other _____	0	1	2	3	4	5
Other _____	0	1	2	3	4	5
Other _____	0	1	2	3	4	5
Other _____	0	1	2	3	4	5

menus and meals department

Your Priorities

Look again at the items in the previous chart that you ranked as a 4 or a 5. Then you and your spouse should read the "I want" statements below and place a check in the box next to the ones that best describe your priorities for managing the Food department in your home. Circle two or three that you each deem most important.

I want ...

his	hers	
❏	❏	to establish healthy eating habits for my family and enjoy tasty, nutritious meals together.
❏	❏	to make meals especially enjoyable times when we share laughter, tears, dreams, and ideas as a family.
❏	❏	to plan menus ahead of time.
❏	❏	to keep our pantry and refrigerator organized and stocked with needed ingredients.
❏	❏	to simplify grocery shopping and shop only once a week.
❏	❏	to use coupons and stretch grocery dollars.
❏	❏	to eat at home more often.
❏	❏	to try new recipes more often.
❏	❏	to make my kitchen more user friendly.
❏	❏	to eat less fast food and more fresh food.
❏	❏	to invite friends or neighbors to share meals with us more often.
❏	❏	to eat breakfast as a family before school and work every morning.
❏	❏	to eat dinner together as a family most nights.
❏	❏	_____
❏	❏	_____
❏	❏	_____
❏	❏	_____

Your Goal

After looking at your priorities, your next step is to write a goal that reflects your desires for this department. For this purpose, a goal is a broad, general, timeless statement that describes your overall aim for this area. Sometimes it is helpful to begin by identifying the key words that you'd use to describe this department when it runs well. Here's an example:

> **Key Words:** *good food, family dinners, snacks for kids, work more as a team*
>
> **Goal:** *To work together to plan menus; prepare tasty, nutritious meals; and eat dinner as a family at least four nights a week; to keep kid-friendly foods on hand so our children and their friends want to be at our home.*

Key Words: _____

_____

Goal: _____

_____

menus and meals department

Using this worksheet, divide up responsibilities for the Menus and Meals department.

Who's Responsible for What?

Responsibilities	Who does it now?	Who else could do it?
Plan meals and menus		
Make the grocery list		
Shop for groceries/supplies		
Shop at wholesale club		
Make breakfast		
Make lunches		
Make dinner		
Clean up after meals		
Make school lunches		
Provide after-school snacks		
Set the table		
Plan and orchestrate dinner parties		
Keep up with coupons		
Feed the baby/young children		
Organize the pantry		
Organize kitchen storage areas		
Keep serving pieces and linens polished and clean		
Prepare for drop-in guests		
Plan and take food to special functions		
Other _____		
Other _____		
Other _____		
Other _____		
Other _____		
Other _____		
Other _____		

five: managing relationships with family and friends

If you've made it this far in the book, you know that the Family Manager system is about creating a smoothly running, low-stress home. It positions you to save money on groceries, juggle after-school schedules, simplify housekeeping routines, plan family celebrations, and fix dripping faucets. The job description of a Family Manager is best summarized in the Family Manager Creed.

The Family Manager Creed

I oversee the most important organization in the world

Where hundreds of decisions are made daily

Where property and resources are managed

Where health and nutritional needs are determined

Where finances and futures are discussed and debated

Where projects are planned and events are arranged

Where transportation and scheduling are critical

Where team building is a priority

I am a Family Manager.

---

relationships trump everything

Note that everything that goes on under the roof of a home is ultimately about the people who live there. Certainly all the Family Manager departments are important, but the Family and Friends department is the one that focuses on tasks related to

GOOD TO KNOW

British children who participated in a study by Luton First said that if children ruled the world, the first thing they would do is ban divorce.

GOOD TO KNOW

Studies show that spending time together as a family boosts children's self-esteem and promotes healthy social development.

relationships—things like holding up your end of your marriage covenant, overseeing the health and education of your children, caring for your aging parents, and staying in touch with friends. The tasks in this department overlap and influence your responsibilities in the other six departments, and vice versa.

For example, take the topic of allowances, which falls in the Finances department. There comes a day in every parent's life when a son or daughter asks, "How come I don't get an allowance?" The way we give our children money and guide their spending opens more than parental purses and wallets—it throws open a family's financial philosophy, budget allotments, values issues, college savings, career prospects, and choices of life partners.

When our firstborn, John, popped the allowance question, I had no ready answer, so I launched into senior manager mode. I promised to get back to my six-year-old and began to research. I scanned current literature and surveyed car pool moms. I sorted through a growing pile of sources (colored tabs were involved) sprouting family-income calculations, age-based equations, and child-rearing philosophies all the way from Dr. James Dobson to my most opinionated single girlfriends.

A few nights later I forced shut my three-ring binder and reported my findings to Bill. He said, "Love, let's just see what makes sense for our family, then set some rules with John." Hmmm. Good idea.

Here's the point. Although a child's allowance is a money issue that is handled through the Finances department, it's also a marriage issue because it requires communication and solidarity—you know, it's one of those "united we stand, divided we fall" issues that you've got to stick together on. It's also a parenting issue because it involves a child's education. A child's allowance helps him or her develop money skills and also signifies that everyone plays on the family team. All this to say, the Family and Friends department is very important—because home and family management involves relationships, and relationships are always most important.

You may find it helpful to look at this as the human resources department of your home. Like any human resources director, you are responsible for "your people"—to promote their physical, spiritual, and mental well-being; to ensure that there are guidelines in place for their protection; and to help them develop their skills and increase their knowledge so they can fulfill their roles well. In short, you must create an environment and orchestrate opportunities that will help each person develop into the best person he or she can be. Managing human resources in your family is the most important part of your Family Manager job description.

But to be clear: managing the Family and Friends department is not about "managing" relationships. It's about managing the tasks that affect your relationships. It's not about calculated manipulation to get other people to do things your way to serve some personal end. It's not about fixing other people or trying to make them into who you think they should be. It's about living with a conscious awareness that your most important job as a wife, mother, daughter, friend, and Family Manager is to build loving, lasting relationships. (This is the most important job for husbands and children as well.) And it's amazing how other things seem to fall into place when you see your most important job as building loving relationships.

This is why you stop organizing your closet, sit down with your husband, and listen to his dreams and frustrations about the future. You make sure you have time alone together, so you block out time on your calendar, secure a sitter, and make reservations for a weekend away. These actions are an important part of building a loving relationship. It's why you read to your children at night and pray with them before bed. It's also why you take them for checkups with the pediatrician and the dentist, and sit on hard bleachers in cold weather to watch their games. Managing the Family and Friends department is about taking care of minds, bodies, and souls.

heed the warning, lose the guilt

This department also comes with a warning: it can produce more stress and guilt than the others—for a couple of reasons. First, you're dealing with human beings who have feelings; and second, a lot of what you do in this department is constantly under scrutiny but, at the same time, is not measurable.

All of us have feelings and needs. We want to feel appreciated and loved. We want to know that others in the world care where we are, what we do, and who we become. Thus, there's a daily tension—a tug between desiring to give of ourselves to others and recognizing the peril of giving ourselves to too many others. So

GOOD TO KNOW

In most American marriages there is no struggle for supremacy, reports the Pew Research Center, because most husbands willingly allow their to wives to make, or at least share equally in, family decisions.

again and again, I personally find the need to study my priorities and decide which people are the most important to me and how much I can give to them.

About the time my life spun out of control and I landed in the hospital (as I mentioned in chapter 2), I realized two truths about priorities and giving. One: setting priorities about time involves setting priorities about people. I admit, I love the feeling of being wanted, and, yes, there were too many people who wanted too many things from me. The second: from that day forward, I was going to have to make some decisions. Some of those decisions would be based on who wanted me, and some would be based on what they wanted. My family took precedence, so I took a leave of absence from the Junior League; I resigned from my position on the women's ministry steering committee at church; and I didn't raise my hand every time the school needed parent volunteers.

Sharing responsibilities with your spouse in the Family and Friends department means working together and separately to protect and nourish the relationships that are most important to you. First and foremost is your marriage—making sure your relationship is vibrant and growing. Next come your children—helping them become the best of who they are intellectually, physically, spiritually, and socially. Then follow relationships with extended family, friends, and neighbors—staying connected and caring as appropriate.

a man's point of view

managing family and friends

"It's business, not personal." When you hear those words, watch out: you've just been put on notice that when maximum profit conflicts with treating people fairly, you lose. I learned in the school of hard knocks to avoid doing business with people who use that phrase. A person who says this is not only telling you something about his priority system, he's also revealing a fundamental misunderstanding of the marketplace. Business *is* personal, because it's all about persons. No persons, no business. Sooner or later, any businessperson who ranks relationships as a low priority will be out of business.

I'd be willing to bet you've never heard anyone say, "It's family, not personal." Although this is no more ignorant than the statement above, we know that family is fundamentally about persons and relationships. But if we're not careful, we can fall into the trap of focusing more on the functions involved in family life—who's going to pay the bills, change the sheets, or mop the kitchen floor—than the ultimate business of family life: creating an environment where human beings love and serve one another so they can grow, flourish, and become all God created them to be.

Many of the tasks in your household could be delegated—but not all of them. If you unexpectedly inherited a fortune and could afford to hire household staff to cover cooking, cleaning, chauffeuring, yard work, maintenance, bookkeeping, scheduling, and event planning, one department includes responsibilities that can't be successfully delegated to outsiders: Family and Friends. No one else can be the husband your wife needs you to be or the father your children need you to be.

Responsibilities in the Family and Friends department revolve around helping those you love develop to their full potential and nurturing relationships between the people in your immediate family, as well as building and maintaining individual and family relationships with other people. Responsibilities related to raising your children, working on your marriage, keeping your extended family together, taking soup to a sick neighbor, and keeping up with old friends and making new ones fall in this department.

Relationships, of course, aren't "things" to be managed. Even so, someone has to take charge of certain tasks related to our children's growth and development, such as enrolling them in preschool, teaching them to ride a bicycle, or quizzing them before a test, for example.

Kathy thinks that Family and Friends may be the most important department of all, and I tend to agree. In some ways this department spawned Kathy's entire Family Manager system. Sure, family management is about making life run smoother, but ultimately it's about building

FROM THE HEART

Never let possessions, positions, or projects become more important than people.

SMART MOVE

Make forgiveness a way of life in your home. Forgiving each other is a lifelong process of canceling the debts of those who fail us again and again. It's not a once-for-all event.

relationships and community. Saving time on housework frees up time for family fun. Saving money on household operations frees up money for a date night. Creating a warm and welcoming home offers family members and friends a place of rest and refreshment from the stress-filled world. Working as a family team provides every member opportunities to bring out the best in one another.

Women get the centrality of this department a lot faster than men, or so it seems. While I've always understood the importance of building relationships, I haven't always connected the dots of what it takes to keep relationships humming. That's why I haven't always understood the importance of things like taking time to talk to my wife about what's frustrating her, even though the big game is on (thank goodness for DVRs), or standing in line (a pet peeve) for two hours with my son to sign him up for baseball. Other responsibilities in this department may include calling your mom and listening to her tell you about her medicine (again), sending your boss a get-well card, taking time during a busy day to encourage a friend, and picking up your neighbor's mail and paper while he's out of town.

Kathy grew up in one place with lifelong friends. Her parents have enjoyed rich friendships with many of the same people for over 50 years—which I believe has a lot to do with their longevity. On the other hand, while growing up, I never lived more than four years in one place. Every time we moved I had to make new friends. Our different upbringings and different views of normal in this department have caused sparks to fly over the years. We've argued about the number of Christmas cards we send (last count: 525), and at times I've been frustrated with all the wedding and graduation gifts we buy. While I'm thinking dollars, Kathy is thinking relationships. Looking back over 38 years of marriage, I'm glad I didn't buck her too much on this issue. We have friends all over the country, many with whom we can pick up right where we left off after several years have passed.

As Kathy mentioned, this department also has the potential to produce more stress and guilt than any other.

We feel social pressure to attend certain functions; we feel family pressure from relatives who expect us to be at *their* home for the holidays; we feel pressure from friends who can't see that they are demanding unrealistic amounts of our time. All of us are limited by time and space, so saying yes to one person always means we're saying no to someone else. One reason it's so important to manage this department well is so we can give the right people the right amount of time and attention they deserve. We simply can't do everything that everyone wants us to do, regardless of the value of their request. And neither will we meet everyone's expectations. And that's okay.

 HIGHLY RECOMMENDED

While many couples never really discuss the depth of their relationships outside immediate family, if you each have different expectations and desires of what these relationships should be, you may run into conflict. Sit down with your wife and complete the His Normal–Her Normal worksheet on page 89. Then take a serious look at your relationships. First, determine which ones are most important. Second, determine what your responsibilities are. Each category—spouse, children, relative, friend— demands a different level of responsibility. How much time do each of you feel you need to devote to each relationship? What is the best way to communicate with each person? The worksheet on page 90 is a great tool to use as you and your wife discuss your relationships.

Taking time to think through this together will pay big dividends.

GOOD TO KNOW

Children gain tremendous security just knowing that Mom and Dad are committed to each other and that their relationship is the most important one in the home. The notion that most children are better off if unhappy parents split up has proven to be false.

SMART MOVE

Don't quarrel in front of your children unless you make a point to let them see you make up.

intimacy: the key to a strong marriage

Intimacy doesn't mean you'll always see eye to eye on everything. Bill and I have put in quite a bit of conflict-resolution time over the years. There have been times when we've come to an impasse in

SMART MOVE

Make a list of things you like about your spouse. Concentrate on these things—not the things that drive you crazy. The size of our character is often measured by the size of the things that annoy us. Overlooking petty irritations is vital to the development of intimacy.

FROM THE HEART

A good marriage is not about expecting my husband or myself to be perfect. It is about cultivating flexibility, patience, understanding, and a sense of humor. It is giving each other an atmosphere in which we can grow.

our relationship and wondered how we'd ever resolve it. Remembering that our marriage vows did not include an exit clause and that we'd committed to giving our children our best, we stuck with it until the problem was solved. These episodes took time and patience, but it was worth every minute, every ounce of energy, and every mustard seed of faith we could muster to resolve them.

Although healthy families are not free of conflict, research has shown that in successful families who raise healthy kids, the parents have a deep connection with one another. This intimacy gives them a reservoir of strength they can draw from to help them cope with problems, resolve conflicts, and face the inevitable crises of life.

Intimacy involves more than physical closeness and emotional transparency. It encompasses our entire being: our minds, emotions, bodies, and spirits.

mental intimacy

Mental intimacy is the meeting and merging of two minds based on mutual respect—a common understanding and esteeming of each other's ideas, thoughts, and values. I'm not implying that a couple must agree on every little point. Bill and I have different opinions about a lot of things. We do, though, agree on the large issues of life and faith.

Mental intimacy is built on communication. One reason so few couples communicate is because they've let other commitments and activities crowd their schedules, leaving scant time for each other. Another reason is that they are seldom alone together. Other people are usually present and interruptive—either in person or via technology.

To grow in mental intimacy, you might start by reading a book together, working on a community service project together, or undertaking another type of project that requires you to exchange ideas, whether landscaping your yard, planting a garden, or learning the language of a country you plan to visit someday.

emotional intimacy

Emotional intimacy is the meeting and merging of two emotional beings based on mutual openness. Emotional intimacy moves beyond opinions to deep feelings. It develops in an atmosphere of understanding and trust as two people share their dreams, fears, experiences, and secrets with one another.

HIS NORMAL—HER NORMAL

family and friends

Consider the conflicts between you and your spouse caused by different ways your families viewed marriage and child rearing, and kept up with extended family and friends when you were growing up. Discuss assumptions that you both brought into your marriage about "normal" ways families maintain relationships. Listen and learn from each other, then negotiate your way to your "new normal" for your relationship. (See examples below.)

His Normal	**Our New Normal**	**Her Normal**
I grew up in a family with lots of cousins. The whole family gathered every Sunday evening at my grandmother's house for dinner. I believe that extended family relationships are valuable and we should get together as much as possible.	We agree that it is important to spend time with our extended families, but we will also set our own schedule and try to achieve balance between time with our immediate family and time with extended family and friends.	I am an only child, and family activities pretty much revolved around me and what I wanted to do. I know developing relationships as a family is important, but I would much rather spend time with my own immediate family and a few friends.
His Normal	**Our New Normal**	**Her Normal**

Relationship Time and Commitment Inventory

As you consider how much time and how high a commitment you want to dedicate to each person or group of people, think in terms of camaraderie, commitment, communication, and connection.

Camaraderie: If you have difficulty connecting with someone, you can't really be friends.

Commitment: Determine what level of relationship you desire and what level of commitment each person or group deserves. In other words, where does each person fit in your priority system when tough decisions must be made about investing your time, energy, or resources?

Communication: Think of the different kinds of communication needed to maintain the level of relationship you desire. For example, we have learned to text our children when we need to ask them a question, but we have to phone our parents. Because these are priority relationships to us, we adapt to the communication style that works best for them.

Connection: Consider when, why, and how often you want to be with a person or group.

Person/Group	Camaraderie	Commitment	Communication	Connection
Spouse				
Children				
Parents				
Siblings				
Extended Family				
Friends				
Other: _____ _____				

Keep Focused on "We," Not "Me"

Bill and I meet a lot of couples who live in two different worlds—the husband engrossed in his and the wife engrossed in hers. Their kids have hit the high school years, and they're together as a couple on expected common grounds—the soccer field, neighborhood barbecues, church on Sunday—but they rarely share, much less pray about, the intricate, life-impacting details of their days and their dreams for the years to come. Their conversations revolve around bills, broken appliances, and who's going to drive the kids to which event. He dreams of getting out of the squirrel cage and playing more golf. She wonders what she's going to do when the kids leave home. She has lived for everyone else for all these years; now it's *her* time. Both of them think in terms of *me*, not *we*.

Maybe you and your spouse have been living separate lives under the same roof. You've been going through the motions of what society expects couples to do, yet your hearts have grown apart, and you're both feeling dissatisfied with life, your relationship, and what the future holds. It doesn't matter who's more to blame. It doesn't matter who's more selfish or who doesn't understand whom. And the truth of the matter is, because God made you husband and wife, one entity to help each other do His will on earth, if God calls either of you to do something, He'll give the other of you a desire to support that dream in some way.

On the whole, women seem to have a much easier time communicating their feelings than men. Many men find it threatening to let down their guard long enough to let someone see into their vulnerable inner person. That's why emotional intimacy grows only in a place of safety. Building trust creates an atmosphere conducive to this level of communication. Criticism, nagging, and anger all stunt the growth of emotional intimacy. No one wants to communicate feelings to someone who is constantly on the offensive. Instead, we must learn to listen carefully and compassionately whenever our mates reveal how they feel.

If listening is a challenge for you, you might try one or more of the following tips:

- Don't interrupt.
- Respond by summarizing what you heard.
- Make eye contact and don't look away when your spouse is speaking.
- If you don't understand something or want more information, ask.

CAUTION!

Revenge is a natural response when someone hurts us; undeserved grace is not. Yet those who do not offer kindness and grace live in various stages of bitterness, guilt, and loneliness. A resentful heart is poisonous. As Anne Lamott puts it: "Not forgiving is like drinking rat poison and then waiting for the rat to die."

CAUTION!

Pay attention to anything that strains or threatens your relationship with your mate.

FROM THE HEART

Author and psychologist Dr. Larry Crabb says two bodies that come together should house two persons who are already together. A couple's sexual relationship does not lead to a good marriage but is the product of a good marriage.

- Pay attention; don't doodle or check messages on your phone.
- Take time to hear the total message. Don't finish your spouse's sentences.
- Don't be in such a hurry to respond that you only think about what you want to say.
- Don't listen to just bits and pieces, because you may draw the wrong conclusion.
- If the discussion is an emotional one, acknowledge your spouse's feelings and show your understanding by saying something like, "I know that must have really hurt you."
- Before you respond, be sure you understand the message.

When it's your turn to speak, remember that emotional intimacy has a vocabulary of its own—made up of words of praise, encouragement, and understanding. This is the language of love. Speak it frequently, and you'll notice emotional oneness developing.

physical intimacy

Physical intimacy is much more than great sex. It's a warm, touching relationship based on mutual affection. Every person has a deep-seated hunger for human contact. We need the physical touch of other living beings. Warm physical affection that is not necessarily a prelude to sex is basic to love and intimacy. Every couple Bill and I have counseled who stopped caring say they stopped touching first.

I've heard many women complain, "The only time he touches me is when he wants to have sex." If this is a problem, talk about it with your spouse. Be specific about when, where, and how you want to be touched. And be patient if one partner is more affectionate than the other. William James, a Harvard psychologist in the late 1800s and early 1900s, said, "The greatest discovery of my generation is that people can alter their lives by altering their attitudes." Dr. James may not have known it, but this great "discovery" is based on Proverbs 23:7: "For as he thinks within himself, so he is" (NASB).

And what was true then is true today. We can alter our lives by altering our attitudes. If you want to change the way you relate to your mate, particularly sexually, you may need to change the way you think about him and the way you think about yourself. Altering your attitude may mean taking care of yourself and your body so

Weekly Quality Time Planner

It's easy to let days and even weeks go by without spending quality time together with your children and spouse. Use this planning sheet to list ways you want to spend time together this week.

DAILY ACTIVITIES	SUPPLIES/PREPARATION NEEDED
Monday	
Tuesday	
Wednesday	
Thursday	
Friday	
Saturday	
Sunday	
Activities with Others	

CAUTION!

Don't have heated discussions in the bedroom. Work through your conflicts in another room and save your bedroom for pleasant moments.

QUICK FIX

QUESTION: *My spouse and I agree that creating intimacy is important, but at this point in our lives, we're lucky if we exchange a quick kiss as we both leave for work in the mornings. Between overseeing dinner and our kids' homework and bedtimes in the evenings, we have little energy left for one another. What do you suggest?*

ANSWER: As unromantic as it may sound, I can testify that what I've done for more than 30 years works. I look at the week ahead and find two likely nights when we can have intimate time as a couple. I try to orchestrate the tasks of those days so I will have energy left at the end of the day for Bill. When the kids were out of school in the summer and their bedtimes were later, they always knew that two nights a week were Mom and Dad's nights and they couldn't stay up as late as usual on those nights. Blocking out times for intimacy doesn't work 100 percent of the time because kids get sick and need to be cared for and other unavoidable circumstances happen, but a 75 to 80 percent success rate is not too bad. And if I didn't make couple time a priority and put it on my calendar (discreetly, of course), it would be too easy for this important part of our relationship to not get the attention it deserves.

you feel more sensual, more ready to connect intimately. It may mean altering the way you communicate so that your mate sees that you're different.

spiritual intimacy

Spiritual intimacy develops as you and your spouse share your spiritual journey, which is based on a mutual dependence on God to meet your deepest longings. Spiritual intimacy provides the atmosphere to describe our deepest thoughts about God and the struggles and joys we experience in becoming the people He created us to be.

In our family, spiritual intimacy begins with faith in Christ and the belief that He absolutely accepts and loves us as we are. Our forgiven position gives us the freedom to serve and encourage each other rather than each demanding that the other make us feel secure and meet our every need. Our relationship really soars when we are aware of God's constant presence in our lives. It gives us the spiritual resources to weather the storms when marriage is less than we hoped and life is harder than we can handle alone. And it gives us the grace to forgive because we are forgiven.

I want to add, however, a word of warning: pushiness can hinder an atmosphere of mutual spiritual growth and cause significant harm to your relationship. Bill and I know many couples whose marriage has deteriorated to passionless cohabitation and some that even ended up in divorce because one partner (usually the wife) nagged the other with a self-righteous smugness about his or her lack of spiritual interest or growth. If you and your spouse are at different places spiritually, be patient and understanding, and take it slow if need be. After all, if you are the one who is leading the spiritual growth initiative (thus, presumably the more spiritual person), remember that your life should be increasingly character-ized by love, joy, peace, patience, kindness, goodness, faithfulness, gentleness, and self-control (see Galatians 5:22-23). Praying for your spouse and living out what you profess to believe, instead of criticizing and condemning, will go a lot further to deepen levels of intimacy in all areas of your relationship.

If you both desire to grow deeper in spiritual intimacy as a couple, perhaps the easiest way to begin your pilgrimage would be to regularly read together. Read a passage from the Bible, a chapter from a good book, or a devotional guide—then talk about your insights. Get up early and begin your day together, or try it just before you go to bed. Listen to audiobooks and sermons in the car together, and discuss what you learn. Or see if there's a couples' Bible study you can join.

The strongest way to build spiritual intimacy is to pray together. Exchange prayer requests so you can pray for each other during the day, and try to spend at least a few minutes praying aloud with each other.

Developing an intimate marriage requires a forgiving heart and calluses on your knees. And like anything worthwhile, intimacy takes commitment, work, and time. In your busy schedule, it isn't

FROM THE HEART

"What do you think the first duty of married people . . . ?"
"Isn't it to help the other to do the will of God?"
—George MacDonald, *The Highlander's Last Song*

Years ago this principle became the anchor of our marriage. We share it with anyone who will listen because we know the tremendous difference it makes to live together in harmony instead of fighting over whose life or calling is more important. God joined us together as husband and wife to do His will and carry forth His Kingdom on planet Earth.

GOOD TO KNOW

Attendance at religious services predicts marital fidelity, according to the *Journal of Marriage and Family*.

CAUTION!

The greatest enemy to a happy marriage is a selfish attitude that is concerned about the other person's character and our own needs instead of vice versa.

likely to happen by accident. For that reason, I recommend that you and your spouse use two helpful worksheets for couples. The first, the Weekly Quality Time Planner, can help you make time for one another throughout the week. (See page 93.) Use the Couple's Questionnaire worksheet on page 97 to discuss how you feel about your place on each other's priority list. And there are lots of simple things you can do to foster intimacy:

- Adjust your schedules so you can go to bed at the same time.
- Pray together before going to sleep.
- Hold hands or lock arms when you are walking.
- Take up some of the slack if your spouse is involved in a big project at work.
- Learn a new skill together: tennis, painting, ballroom dancing, or square dancing.
- Start a dream file. Clip pictures of things you both love: a vacation spot, a house, a cabin on a lake, a painting.
- Read quietly together.
- Write a poem, a song, or a love letter to your mate.
- Invite your spouse on a business trip.
- Honor each other's occasional need for solitude.
- Show genuine interest in each other's world.
- Keep pictures of the two of you together on your desk and around the house.
- Learn about something your spouse is interested in so you can discuss the topic with enthusiasm.
- Don't raise your voice, even in a heated argument.
- Begin each day with a positive greeting and a smile.
- Check with your spouse before changing plans that involve both of you.
- Offer a thirst-quenching beverage in the middle of a tedious job.
- Say, "I love you" often.
- Compliment your spouse when you're alone and when you're in front of others.
- Never criticize your spouse in front of others.
- Help each other reach a personal goal.
- Make a list of the ways you would like your spouse to express love to you. Ask your spouse to do the same, and then exchange lists. Encourage each other to go on retreats. Offer to cover home base.

Building Intimacy: A Couple's Questionnaire

In every marriage, priorities get out of line now and then. Use this form to talk about your feelings and discuss ways you can put your marriage at the top of the list of what's most important. Please answer the following questions honestly. Say how you really feel, not what you think your spouse wants to hear. How important do you feel?

For Wives

1. I feel more or less important to my husband than . . .

   Write "+" if you feel more important than what is listed.
   Write "−" if you feel less important than what is listed.
   Write "=" if you feel equally as important as what is listed.

   _____ his work
   _____ his computer/cell phone
   _____ his friends
   _____ his rest
   _____ his hobbies

   _____ his faith
   _____ his church
   _____ his yard
   _____ his outside activities or meetings
   _____ our children/extended family

2. I would feel more important to my husband if I could _____ .

3. I would feel more important to my husband if he would _____ .

4. I feel really proud of myself when I _____ .

5. I am really good at _____ .

6. I really enjoy _____ .

7. I feel worthless when I _____ .

8. If I could change one thing about myself, it would be _____ .

For Husbands

1. I feel more or less important to my wife than . . .

   Write "+" if you feel more important than what is listed.
   Write "−" if you feel less important than what is listed.
   Write "=" if you feel equally as important as what is listed.

   _____ her work
   _____ her computer/cell phone
   _____ her friends
   _____ her rest
   _____ her hobbies

   _____ her faith
   _____ her church
   _____ her yard
   _____ her outside activities or meetings
   _____ our children/extended family

2. I would feel more important to my wife if I could _____ .

3. I would feel more important to my wife if she would _____ .

4. I feel really proud of myself when I _____ .

5. I am really good at _____ .

6. I really enjoy _____ .

7. I feel worthless when I _____ .

8. If I could change one thing about myself, it would be _____ .

- Attend a marriage enrichment conference.
- Agree to never go to bed angry.
- Get away without the kids at least twice a year.

parenting as a team

When Bill and I became parents, we read everything we could about child rearing by all sorts of authors. We collected a notebook full of ideas and strategies but kept coming back to three particular principles from Aristotle. An ancient Greek philosopher is usually not the first person you'd think of when asked to come up with a child expert, but for us as parents who had a lot to teach and communicate to our children, we thought his philosophy made a lot of sense. Aristotle summarized three components of effective teaching and communication: *logos* (content), *ethos* (character), and *pathos* (compassion).

Here's what I think each means for us as parents today:

1. We must provide evidence that the message we are teaching is relevant to daily living. It's important that we communicate the logos—the content of the truth—in practical ways so our kids can see the logic and reason behind it. The truth we want them to learn must be woven into the fabric of everyday conversation and family life. This should be done formally in age-appropriate learning moments and informally in teachable moments when you can reaffirm the truth.

   Take time soon to think about what values you want your children to take with them when they leave home, then look for everyday ways to inculcate those values. For example, if you want your children to understand what true heroism is, you might read a portion of the book of Esther after dinner and then point out a story that happened to be in the news that day to further illustrate the point. It's also a good idea to envision your son or daughter one, five, and ten years from now, then, as a couple, write developmental goals for each of your children. What opportunities can you orchestrate to enhance their intellectual, physical, spiritual, and social development? Use the Development Goals worksheet on page 99 to give structure to your ideas. Doing this will help you be alert for formal and informal opportunities to nudge them toward these goals.

GOOD TO KNOW

What we leave *in* our children is far more important than what we leave *to* them.

CAUTION!

We are living models for our children. What we are communicates far more than what we say. There's little point in teaching what we do not practice.

Child Development Goals

Sharing parenting responsibilities begins with shared goals. Spend time discussing the unique talents and giftedness of each of your children. Set goals for how you want to see them develop during the school year or the summer. (See example in top boxes.)

	INTELLECTUAL	PHYSICAL	SPIRITUAL	SOCIAL
Name: Alissa				
Goals:	Study abroad for a semester	Try out for tennis team in March; make the team	Grow in faith; join youth group	Grow in self-confidence when at dress-up events
Ideas:	Talk with French teacher; research foreign-exchange programs online	Practice at the park court two times a week; contact YMCA about lessons	Ask friends for church recom-mendations; contact Young Life office for ideas	Check into etiquette class at department store; Dad to teach Alissa how to waltz
Name:				
Goals:				
Ideas:				
Name:				
Goals:				
Ideas:				
Name:				
Goals:				
Ideas:				

FROM THE HEART

Evaluate your own spiritual journey and consider what your children are learning about faith from you. Ask yourself honestly if what you believe adequately covers the serious issues of life. Does your faith give your life meaning, purpose, and peace? Does your faith support you in every phase of living: youth, young adulthood, middle age, old age, marriage crises, financial crises, children's crises, energy crises, cultural crises, and moral crises? Does it offer a healthy way to deal with guilt and forgiveness? Does it answer the question of evil and still give you hope? Does it provide a way for you to look realistically at the problems of life without despair? I encourage you to come to terms with these questions—for your own sake and your children's.

2. Who we are is more important than what we say. Our greatest leverage in teaching our children is our ethos, or character. What we teach them (and they're learning something from us, whether we like it or not) must be more than merely passing on facts and information. It must be an overflow of our lives. When the principles and values we're teaching match how we're living, our kids will have trust in us as teachers.

For example, if we want our children to understand that the Ten Commandments are not just suggestions, we must strive to obey them ourselves. Let's say that when you return something at a department store, the clerk makes an error and gives you back more money than you paid for the item. Just as you've taught your kids the eighth commandment, "You must not steal," you point out the error and give back the extra money without a second thought.

3. Our children must know that we love them unconditionally. Pathos, or compassion, has to do with our emotions and feelings. As parents, we must try to understand and care about the emotional makeup of our children—as well as their intellectual and spiritual beings. All are critically important.

Children want to know they are loved unconditionally. In a world where performance means everything, kids need to know the tryouts are over at home. They've already made our team—and nothing they do will cause us to cut them from our lineup.

Parents who send their child the message that their love is conditional and based on behavior—"I love you if you make the honor roll," "I love you if you score a goal and don't embarrass me," "I love you if you weigh 115 pounds"—harm their child and their relationship with the child.

When our children sense that we love them unconditionally, are trying to understand their feelings, and have compassion toward them, they are motivated to learn what we want them to learn and do what we want them to do. On the other hand, they will not accept our values if they don't value their relationship with us.

Children must know that we value them as uniquely designed individuals—because they are. That's why there's no such thing as standardized parenting. We must approach each of our children as a one-of-a-kind person, seeking to understand how he or she is individually wired and how to nurture that child accordingly. We need to know their unique characteristics, such as their learning styles—if they learn best by listening, watching, or doing—and whether they are left-brain or right-brain dominant. We need to know whether they perform better individually or on a team, what kinds of rewards motivate them, and what type of discipline is most effective.

One of the worst things we can do to a child is to try to fit him or her into a mold of our own making or compare him in a derogatory way to a sibling. Another danger parents must avoid is ignoring or downplaying the threats posed by exploding technology. (See the sidebar on page 102.)

ideas for quality time with your kids

Most parents understand the importance of regularly spending quality time with their children. Many, however, say that when time opens up, they can't think of what to do. The list below may be helpful when you find yourself in a similar situation.

If you have only 10 to 15 minutes:

- Play a round or two of Boggle or Wii. Keep a running score.
- Sit in *their* room and talk.
- Read a book or listen to them read to you (be sure and ask questions so they know you are really listening).
- Show your child how to yo-yo.
- Use toothpicks to roast miniature marshmallows by candlelight.
- Take a quick walk outside, pointing out unique things about the particular season.
- Make up a silly story together.
- Fix a snack, maybe even invent one, and sit down together to enjoy it.
- Look at their recent schoolwork and have them tell you about what they are learning (this isn't the time to be critical, just interested).
- Play catch.

CAUTION!

Don't set an agenda for your child's life. Whether it's excelling at sports, earning high grades, or choosing a particular vocation, forcing a child to fit a mold of your making—one that doesn't consider how God designed the child—is a sure path to frustration for both of you. It also sets up a natural conflict. If your child fails to live up to your agenda, he or she will naturally feel estranged from your love.

A New and Present Danger

As a Facebook newbie, I've enjoyed connecting with old friends and people who have just discovered Family Manager Coaching and resources. But last year I endured a lengthy battle with a hacker who violated my Facebook account. Getting hacked again and again by someone who used my Facebook persona to send out video links to pornography was beyond frustrating. This horrific experience launched me into research mode about Internet safety and the dangers of Internet pornography and predators. What I learned made me want to launch a cross-country "get out the message" campaign, because all parents need to know and act on what I learned to keep their children safe.

- Nine out of 10 children have been accidentally exposed to online pornography.
- The average age of exposure to pornography is seven years old (some studies say five years old).
- 20 percent of teens admit to participating in "sexting" (sending or receiving sexually explicit text or images) by cell phone.
- 20 percent of teens say they have sent or posted nude or seminude pictures or videos of themselves.
- 39 percent of teens say they send or post sexually suggestive messages.
- 48 percent of teens say they have received sexually suggestive messages.
- 44 percent of teens say it is common for sexually suggestive text messages to be shared with people other than the intended recipient.
- 36 percent of teen girls and 39 percent of teen boys say it is common for nude or seminude photos to be shared with people other than the intended recipient.
- 33 percent of online solicitations of minors occur via social networking sites.
- 32 percent of online teens have been contacted by strangers online.

Please, please don't take this lightly. Don't think this is about someone else's child. Your family is not immune, and you need to protect your children—today. First, you should be aware of the key signs that your child may be interacting with inappropriate online content. They include:

1. Your child spends large amounts of time online, especially at night.
2. You find inappropriate images or files on your child's computer.
3. Your child receives or makes phone calls to numbers you don't recognize.
4. Your child receives mail, gifts, or packages from someone you don't know.
5. Your child turns the computer monitor off or quickly changes the screen on the monitor when you approach.
6. Your child withdraws from the family.
7. Your child is using an account that belongs to someone else.[1]

As a parent, you need to monitor the online activity of your children and teens, whether or not you have observed any of the suspicious behavior above. After researching the best way to do this, I recommend reviewing and then installing parental control software. (My personal favorite is the award-winning Safe Eyes program.) Look for a program that will:

- allow children to participate in social networking safely
- instantly alert you if a child receives or sends a suspicious message or visits a suspicious Web site
- monitor when and how long children are on the Internet
- keep track of children's text-messaging usage and habits

---

[1] Federal Bureau of Investigation, "A Parent's Guide to Internet Safety," http://www.fbi.gov/publications/pguide/pguidee.htm.

- Draw a picture together.
- Write a letter to the president. Ask him to send you a book about the White House.

If you have 30 minutes to one hour:

- Play a favorite board game like checkers or Monopoly.
- Play the "favorite things" game. Ask each other questions like "What's my favorite color?" and see how many each of you can answer correctly without help.
- Work a small puzzle.
- Create toothpick architecture. Roll modeling clay into small beads, about one-quarter inch in diameter, and use them as corner joints for the toothpicks.
- Go on a short drive to a favorite drink spot or ice cream store.
- Play balloon volleyball. Tie a string between two chairs for a net.
- Preserve a spiderweb. Find an abandoned spiderweb and dust it gently with talcum powder. Place a piece of black construction paper in a cardboard box; coat the paper with hair spray. While the hair spray is slightly tacky, mount the web onto the paper. Coat the paper with acrylic spray to preserve the web.
- Make a homemade card together that you can mail to someone special.
- Work together on a project for someone else, like sweeping an elderly neighbor's porch.
- Go on a bike ride or exercise together at home.
- Fix a meal together.
- Visit the Web sites of states you would like to visit, collecting information about fun things to do and interesting places to go there.
- Make puzzles. Tape a row of popsicle sticks together, then turn over and draw a picture. Remove tape and mix them up to solve the puzzle.

If you have two hours:

- Help your child fix a bike or toy.
- Make your own "lick 'em, stick 'em" stickers with a young child. Mix 2 teaspoons white glue with 1 teaspoon white vinegar. Cut out photos from magazines or draw fun pictures.

TECH TIP

Shazam is an iPhone app that allows you to identify whatever song is playing in the background wherever you are. You can record a sound bite from a song your child says he or she loves and get details to help you decide if the lyrics line up with your family's listening values.

Brush the backs of the pictures with the mixture and let dry. Then lick and stick.

- Come up with a list of about 20 questions, and interview your child as if you were a reporter. Record the interview, listen to it together, and then send copies to grandparents.
- Watch your child's favorite movie as you snuggle together.
- Make salt sculptures. Mix together 4 cups flour, 1½ cups water, and 1 cup salt. Sculpt dough into animals, flowers, rockets, etc. Bake at 350 degrees for one hour. Cool and paint with acrylic paint if desired. Brainstorm how this medium might be a good one for an entry in the school art show or science fair.
- Make sock puppets from old socks and leftover buttons, craft supplies, or paint pens. Then put on a puppet show.
- Form a "business." Create a logo, mission statement, and letterhead.
- Work on a scrapbook together. Get an old photo album or make your own by folding several sheets of scrapbook paper in half and stapling or sewing down the middle. Pick one event to cover and then insert a few pictures in the scrapbook, along with notes about the when, where, why, who, and what of the occasion you're covering.
- Go through the house collecting all the change you can find. Then sort and roll it in coin wrappers, or count it and start a money jar.
- Build a model plane or car from a kit.
- Go to the top of the tallest building in your area and look for landmarks.
- Buy small used appliances at a secondhand store to take apart and put back together.

Ways to spend quality time with teenagers:

- Take them to a coffee shop and talk.
- Play a card game together.
- Take a walk together.
- Help them organize a closet or the area under their bed without griping about the mess.
- Make a babysitter's kit together that your teen can take along when babysitting. Include fun activities, first aid information,

a list of questions to ask the parents, and basic discipline techniques. Make business cards together on your computer.

- Spread out a blanket and have lunch or a snack on their bedroom floor (like an indoor picnic—just don't call it that).
- Ask them to teach you something new about technology, such as how to blog or create a LinkedIn profile.
- Roll socks into sock balls, clear an area of breakables, and have a sock war.
- Research the Internet for fun recipes to make together. Start her or his own recipe book.
- Help your teen make a résumé and conduct a pretend interview.
- Research a charity your teen is interested in and help him or her create a plan to donate time or money to the organization. Write down goals and actually see them through.

learning from each other

Even if both parents are excellent teachers, providing good content and exhibiting character and compassion, unless we communicate our messages from a position of humility, our children will probably not value our "pearls of wisdom." Just because we're the adults doesn't mean we're always right. We are learners, just like our children. Sure, we want to stay one step ahead of our kids, but we must never forget that we are still en route and have a long way to go.

Parents who believe they have to be right all the time will have real problems with their children. They don't fool anyone but themselves when they try to come across as experts or people who have arrived. We can get away with this kind of attitude—sort of—when kids are young, but not with teenagers. They can smell a phony a mile away.

If we admit we are not always right, the obvious corollary is that we can be wrong. In my case, I am often wrong. I try to remember the importance of communicating my imperfection to my children. A young mom told me that she didn't want her mom to help out after her baby was born because she never had a close relationship with her mom. Why? Her mom has never been willing to say, "I was wrong."

Criticism is another toxin that works its way into many families. When we dwell on our children's shortcomings, it's easy to overlook the wonderful things we love about them. If you sense you may have hurt your child, take a step back, look deeper inside yourself, and

GOOD TO KNOW

The average child today spends 45 hours a week with some form of media, compared with just 30 hours in school, according to researchers from Yale and the National Institutes of Health. Nielsen Online reports that the fastest growing group of Internet users is children ages two to eleven.

CAUTION!

"I get many letters from you parents about your children. You want to know why we people up here in Princeton can't make more out of them and do more for them. Let me tell you the reason we can't. It may shock you just a little, but I am not trying to be rude. The reason is that they are your sons, reared in your homes, blood of your blood, bone of your bone. They have absorbed the ideals of your homes. You have formed and fashioned them. They are your sons. In those malleable, moldable years of their lives, you have forever left your imprint upon them."

—Woodrow Wilson, when he was president of Princeton University

seek to discover whether your criticism may have wounded him or her. Ask yourself some tough questions, such as:

- Is there anything I might have done to unjustly offend my child?
- Have I been unreasonable in my expectations about our home, schedules, or how I want to be treated?
- Have I been critical or judgmental?
- Have I been impatient or rude?
- Have I shown compassion and unconditional love?
- Have I *really* listened and tried to understand why my child is upset with me?

Bill and I have witnessed many parents—including ourselves—making a lot of mistakes. It has been reassuring to see that children are amazingly resilient to parental mistakes—if the parents are willing to admit their mistakes and offer a sincere apology. But the rigid inability to say, "I was wrong; would you forgive me?" does irreparable damage between parent and child.

staying connected to friends

One thing Bill and I have learned over the years is that as a married couple, our spouse is our best friend. The marriage covenant between a man and a woman creates restricted air space. It is a "no fly" zone for anyone else, including parents, children, friends—anyone. Besides your relationship with God, no person or thing is to have more importance in your life than your spouse. That said, friends are important for you and your spouse, individually and as a couple.

Someone recently commented to me that Bill and I have a lot of friends. I've never sat down to count our friends, but that observation made me think of how very blessed we are to have friends across the country, in other countries, and in every place we've lived. We also have friends from college days and from every stage of our family's life. A few of our friends we see fairly regularly, but we don't get to see most as often as we would like, and we see some hardly ever, though we still care about them, pray for them, and communicate with them occasionally.

In chapter 2 I talked about how managing our time has a lot to

QUICK FIX

QUESTION: *What's an easy way to stay connected with extended family members and friends who live far away?*

ANSWER: You will make anyone feel special and remembered if you send him or her a birthday card with a personal note. To make this process simple, pick up an accordion file with monthly dividers at an office supply store. Make up a list of birthdays you'd like to remember according to their months. Keep that list in the front of the file. Then take a few hours one weekend to purchase cards (they can be bought more inexpensively in bulk) and address them. Jot the birthday in pencil where you'll eventually place the stamp. Then sort them by month and store them in the file. Once or twice a month, pull out the cards for that month. Sign, stamp, and seal them before taking the batch to be mailed.

While this is a simple process, even this may seem overwhelming; if so, there's nothing wrong with acknowledging a birthday with an e-card.

Many families stay connected with extended family and friends by sending a newsletter at Christmas, summarizing the goings-on in their family since the last December. You might consider creating an e-newsletter to send out when school gets out for the summer that recaps the school year or just before it starts again with highlights of your summer or on a family member's birthday to give loved ones and special friends an update.

do with the rhythm of our lives. This concept applies to friendships, too. There are simply times in life when we have more time for friends than other times, because our lives are constantly in flux. Certain seasons in our family's life and hectic times in our personal life make it impossible to connect with our friends as much as we would like. At other times we can give a lot of ourselves to our friends, and at times they give a lot of themselves to us. The reality of friendships is that they ebb and flow. And perhaps one way to know if a friend is really a friend is if he or she understands this.

GOOD TO KNOW

The more happy people you know, the more likely you are to be happy yourself, according to a report in the *British Medical Journal*. People with the most social connections—friends, spouses, neighbors, relatives—are also the happiest. Each additional connection makes you happier.

SMART MOVE

As a family, read a portion of the book of Proverbs every day at breakfast or dinner. Have a child record an ongoing list of all the characteristics of true friendship that you come across. This will teach them (and remind you) how to be a good friend and to know if someone is a good friend to them.

Some couples say that they each have friends from work, the neighborhood, or through clubs and organizations, but they don't have many couple friends—and they struggle to know how to connect with other like-minded couples. Here are some ways to start the process of forging friendships together.

- Organize a block party, coordinate a neighborhood-wide garage sale, or start a crime-watch committee for your street to get to know your neighbors.
- Volunteer as a couple at a school function, community organization program, or political campaign.
- Strike up conversations with other parents on the sidelines of your kids' games and practices.
- Join a church and attend a couples' Sunday school class.
- Get into tailgating. Connect with friends from college or make new friends in your community as you cheer your alma mater or local football team to victory. Tailgating is a great way to forge new friendships. Get to know your parking-lot neighbors and enjoy their company while waiting for traffic to clear after the game. It's a perfect way to end a full day of fun.
- Start a couples' book club or bunco club at your home with couples you've met and would like to get to know better.
- Go on a couples' retreat sponsored by your church or another organization. For suggestions, see pages 205–206 in the Web Resources section.
- Invite one or more couples over to your home for dinner. To get the conversation going, ask everyone, starting with you or your spouse, to share their answers to the following questions:

   If you could travel back in time, what period of history would you like to experience firsthand?
   What are your three favorite films of all time?
   What's the best book you've ever read?
   If you could eat dinner with three people, who would you choose?

Now that you've considered some ways to strengthen your relationships with your spouse, children, and friends, what steps should you take first? Be sure to work through the ACT worksheets that begin on page 110.

THE MOST IMPORTANT THINGS TO REMEMBER

1. The highest calling of every member of your family is to help one another do the will of God.

2. The family is the most important organization in the world, and building loving, lasting relationships is the most important job you'll ever have. When you make this your priority, other things seem to fall into place.

3. The ultimate business of family life is creating an environment in which human beings love and serve one another so they can grow, flourish, and become all God created them to be.

4. Sharing responsibilities in the Family and Friends department means working together and separately to protect and nourish the relationships that are most important to you as a couple.

5. A good marriage doesn't just happen. Rather, spouses who cultivate flexibility, patience, understanding, and a sense of humor build a good marriage. In this atmosphere, each of them can grow.

6. Children gain tremendous security just knowing Mom and Dad are committed to each other and that theirs is the most important relationship in the house.

7. A family is on-site training for growing human beings to learn how to care for a wide variety of emotional and physical pains by receiving loving care and by watching it being given to others.

8. You and your spouse must work together to intentionally teach your children the values you want them to embrace. Otherwise societal forces will answer their questions about their identity, parameters for right and wrong, and what's important in life—and you may not like the answers they provide.

9. The small acts of love you show daily will, over time, add up to big differences that often cannot be seen today.

10. The family is God's invention. He knows best how to make it work.

family and friends department

Take a few minutes to think about the key causes of stress in the Family and Friends department of your home. You and your spouse should use a different color pen or pencil to circle the number that best describes your individual stress level for each topic.

Key: 1=No Stress; 5=Very Stressful (0=Not Applicable)

Parenting	0	1	2	3	4	5
Family communication	0	1	2	3	4	5
Kids' disobedience	0	1	2	3	4	5
Bickering among kids	0	1	2	3	4	5
Marriage issues	0	1	2	3	4	5
Family fun	0	1	2	3	4	5
Adjustment to new baby	0	1	2	3	4	5
Child care	0	1	2	3	4	5
Kids at home alone	0	1	2	3	4	5
School success	0	1	2	3	4	5
Kids' homework	0	1	2	3	4	5
Teaching kids manners	0	1	2	3	4	5
Blended family issues	0	1	2	3	4	5
Extended family issues	0	1	2	3	4	5
Keeping up with friends	0	1	2	3	4	5
Extended family in your home	0	1	2	3	4	5
Adult children in your home	0	1	2	3	4	5
Teaching kids right and wrong	0	1	2	3	4	5
Parenting teenagers	0	1	2	3	4	5
Television/computer time	0	1	2	3	4	5
Internet safety for kids	0	1	2	3	4	5
Summer schedule/activities	0	1	2	3	4	5
Children's spiritual growth	0	1	2	3	4	5
Other _____	0	1	2	3	4	5
Other _____	0	1	2	3	4	5
Other _____	0	1	2	3	4	5
Other _____	0	1	2	3	4	5
Other _____	0	1	2	3	4	5
Other _____	0	1	2	3	4	5
Other _____	0	1	2	3	4	5
Other _____	0	1	2	3	4	5

family and friends department

Your Priorities

Look again at the items in the previous chart that you ranked as a 4 or a 5. Then you and your spouse should read the "I want" statements below and place a check in the box next to the ones that best describe your priorities for the Family and Friends department in your home. Circle two or three that you individually deem most important.

I want . . .

his	hers	
❏	❏	to always remember that relationships are the most important thing in life—that people are more important than projects.
❏	❏	to learn how to love my family in ways they can understand.
❏	❏	to help my children develop to their full potential mentally, physically, spiritually, socially, and emotionally.
❏	❏	to help my spouse succeed in his/her career.
❏	❏	to make dates with my spouse a priority.
❏	❏	to foster an all-for-one, one-for-all team spirit in our family.
❏	❏	to be a good friend to my friends.
❏	❏	to keep up with our extended family.
❏	❏	to remember the birthdays of people we care about.
❏	❏	to promote health and wellness in our family.
❏	❏	to enhance my parenting skills.
❏	❏	to learn to communicate in more effective ways with family members.
❏	❏	to be prepared for medical emergencies and disasters.
❏	❏	to get involved as a family at our place of worship.
❏	❏	_____
❏	❏	_____
❏	❏	_____
❏	❏	_____

Your Goal

Consider your individual and shared priorities, then write an overall goal that reflects your desires for the Family and Friends department. For this purpose, think of a goal as a broad, general, timeless statement that describes your overall aim for this department. Sometimes it is helpful to begin by identifying the key words that you'd use to describe this department when it runs well. Here's an example:

Key Words: *relationships, develop, potential, stay connected*

Goal: *To remember that relationships are more important than anything else; to help our children and each other develop to our God-given potential; to stay connected in meaningful ways to extended family and friends we care about.*

Key Words: _____

_____

Goal: _____

_____

family and friends department

Using this worksheet, divide up responsibilities for the Family and Friends department.

Who's Responsible for What?

Responsibilities	Who does it now?	Who else could do it?
Research/arrange child care		
Dress/transport young children		
Bathe young children		
Research/register kids for school		
Read to the kids		
Put the kids to bed		
Plan creative outings/activities with kids		
Volunteer/participate in school events		
Participate in school and other events with children		
Purchase school supplies		
Help with homework		
Drop off and pick up kids from school		
Research/register kids for activities/lessons		
Transport kids to after-school activities		
Meet with teachers		
Teach children values		
Teach children manners/social skills		
Administer discipline		
Monitor television, music, and the Internet		
Take kids to physician and dentist appointments		
Care for small children		
Schedule playdates		
Oversee college testing/application process		
Visit potential colleges		
Arrange family outings		
Plan date nights with spouse		
Care for aging family members		
Keep up with extended family		
Keep up with friends		
Send gifts to relatives and friends		
Send greeting cards		
Write thank-you notes		
Care for pets		
Oversee relationships with neighbors		
Other _____		
Other _____		
Other _____		
Other _____		

six: managing your finances

Family Managers must be infinitely creative with finite income. You've got to pay the bills and stretch the dollars that remain, hold back debt while adding to your savings—challenging tasks all, but especially during economic downturns.

If you're feeling fidgety and want to reach for a book on a topic less torturous, like quantum physics, that only proves you have a pulse and a Social Security number. Money talk ignites fears and provokes emotions. Yet tackling financial issues, even tough ones, can strengthen family bonds. Shared goals for money and spending can lift thinking and more firmly connect husbands, wives, and children.

When it comes to choosing what you want out of life, making choices as a team can strengthen your marriage—not to mention preserve your assets. Trust me: until both you and your spouse walk one financial path, you'll make regrettable decisions and wind up using words you can't undo by hitting rewind.

Step one, the most essential, is to uncover two sets of values: yours and your mate's. Few people are married to their financial twin. Until you know, really *know*, what each of you holds dear—and from that list identify the values you share as a couple—you'll lose your way.

the danger of unsettled values

Recently, a stay-at-home mom (I'll call her Lisa to honor her privacy) told me that she and her husband, Jack, never had a serious conversation about what was most important to them. During the

GOOD TO KNOW

Tightwads tend to marry spendthrifts, according to researchers at the University of Michigan. Yet couples with opposing views toward spending are more likely to argue over money and be less satisfied with their marriages. If spending decisions are causing friction in your marriage, taking time to develop a financial philosophy you can both agree on is an investment worth making.

CAUTION!

Don't make financial decisions (or any other important decisions) while you're scrambling to get the kids dressed and to school on time or rushing to a ball game. Vital decisions deserve your focused time and attention. Schedule a time to address them when you can do so without interruptions.

early years of their marriage, the couple owned an older home about 10 minutes from Jack's workplace in Dallas. After their first child was born, Lisa attended a baby shower for a former coworker in a fast-growing outlying suburb. She fell in love with the neighborhood and the idea of having a new home with new appliances. She sold Jack on the idea of selling their home and moving out of the city by suggesting that they use part of the money they would make on the sale of their existing home to buy him a new car with a fancy stereo system. (This was in 2005, at the peak of the housing market.)

As planned, they sold their old house and bought a new one, along with a new car. However, the excitement over their new house with new appliances and Jack's new car with the great sound system was short lived—for at least two reasons. First, Jack's commute now consumed two hours a day, give or take a little, depending on traffic. Second, seven months after their move, Lisa gave birth to twins, and she needed Jack to be home more—not less. After three years of blaming each other for the move, their marriage was crumbling. They had not considered that moving would mean less time to work on building a strong marriage and family life, something they both desired but never articulated. Because they had never verbalized their life goals to one another, they hadn't thought through the impact a move to the suburbs would make on what they valued most. Now they were close to losing an invaluable relationship because they had never talked about what they truly valued.

What do you and your spouse value? The right address, maybe? Moving up, expanding your network? Or not. (Some people arrive at what they value by eliminating what they don't value.) Education? Maybe recreation, the out-of-doors, living near the mountains or coast, caring for your parents, a beautiful home, children, collecting art, an unusual hobby, music, friends, travel abroad, classic cars, working with teens or refugees, faith and church, political activism? None of these is a moral issue in and of itself; pursuing any of them requires a personal judgment call. Only you can know your attachment to a given value and how you would feel should first things fall out of first place. Keeping first things at the front of the line is the key to both advancement and contentment.

Years ago a wise older mom said to me, "Kathy, if you have to move one inch from where you are right now to be happy, you never will be content." Over and over in my life, her words have rung true and, in difficult times, have helped me calibrate my thinking. It's an interesting word, *contentment*. It means you find your joy in the now; you're as happy here as you would be there. For decades Americans have rushed past the here for the there: the new house, the updated kitchen, the workout or weight-loss or self-improvement program, the car, the name-drop vacation or second home, the latest GPS device, plasma TV, video game, or digital distraction.

Is it "settling for less" to be content? No. It's wise. It means you know your values and you're living in them. It also means that you're living deliberately.

what does money mean to you?

Early in our marriage Bill and I began the conversation about our family financial philosophy, and it's a talk that's still in progress—both so we can pass it on to our kids and so we can stay close to the line and to each other.

One of the first things we learned was that our individual definitions of *need* and *want* were deeply ingrained and wildly relative concepts. Bill and I come from drastically different backgrounds with divergent views on earning, saving, spending, and giving money. When we were setting up our first home, those differences rose up and messed with our relationship: how much to spend on item X—or not; our perceptions of quality; our views of needs versus wants; and plenty more. Not long after that we had children—and, oh boy, *then* did our backgrounds throw up walls.

I was reared in an upper-middle-class world where in the summers all responsible parents enrolled their four-year-olds in private swimming lessons at the country club. Children saw the dentist twice a year, got braces when their adult teeth came in, and attended camp from first grade on. In my world, a teen got a driver's license and a new car on the same day, and parents paid for whatever college their children chose.

In the frugal world of Bill's childhood, kids got necessities and few extras. Fads in new toys or bikes came and went without his needing to have one. He learned to swim at the public pool and as a teen had to earn his own spending money. He got his first car his junior year of college, and he paid for gas from the money he earned as a part-time school bus driver. As for paying for college,

FROM THE HEART

The Finances department may make more sense to you and your spouse when you see that in some ways it's like running a business partnership. You need to make a budget and keep track of earnings, expenses, and debts. When it comes to making big financial decisions and setting goals, do it together. Even when your decisions backfire or you fall short of your goals or you encounter unexpected financial calamity, you'll weather the crisis better by walking through it together.

GOOD TO KNOW

Most couples
(64 percent) merge
their money into
joint accounts when
they get married,
according to a study
conducted by *Smart-
Money* and *Redbook*
magazines. The
report also found
that more than 70
percent of spouses
talk to their partners
about money at least
once a week.

well, scholarships and financial aid drove that bus. And yet he never felt deprived. It was the system he learned in the loving home where he was raised.

Because of our different perspectives, many of our first financial discussions kindled emotions and fueled insecurity. We saw first-hand how money has the power to destroy relationships that are infinitely more valuable than material riches. We made a commitment to keep communicating and negotiating our way to common ground and financial tenets that would define our lifestyle. Over the years, little of our original philosophy has changed. Some directions have shifted with the size and age of our family, but we both know due north.

your family financial policy

If you think about it, every family has a financial policy, written or unwritten, even if it's a policy to live in chaos and make it up as they go along. Yet every family needs a well-conceived financial policy—the guardrails that keep a couple on the same route going up the mountain. Following are the principles—the beliefs that came from our thinking separately and together—that inform the Peel family financial policy.

1. *Responsibility.* Taking care of things is not only wise stewardship; it's a smart move financially. As I came to learn, cars last longer when you change the oil every 3,000 miles. Like the mechanic comparing a $25 oil change to a $4,500 engine replacement: "Pay me now or pay me later."

2. *Personal productivity.* From the beginning, Bill and I were in lockstep on the work ethics we each inherited. If something we wanted was outside our budget, we brainstormed ways to earn extra income—tutor, house-sit, start another home-based business. When our family changed houses, we found do-it-yourself moving options. We bought used furniture and refinished or reupholstered it ourselves. We bought home repair books and got handy with wallpaper, fixtures, and even the mysterious region under the sink. Saving money became a game, and we liked wearing the same jersey.

3. *Honesty.* Here's another one Bill and I both grew up on: honesty is the only policy. Nothing worth having is worth fibbing or fudging to get.

4. *Generosity.* It was Winston Churchill who said, "We make a living by what we get, but we make a life by what we give." We knew we wanted to live with open hands and be a family of givers, and we brainstormed ways to do it.

5. *Personal identity.* We are not what we own, wear, or drive. If a fad, fashion, or activity becomes a must, a red flag goes up in our minds right away. Bill and I both believe character is identity; when we allow circumstances to mold us into lesser versions of ourselves, that's the touchstone we return to.

6. *Relational equity.* Spending time and/or money to build relationships and create shared memories is a good investment. Think of it as dollar cost averaging for your marriage or relationship with a child, where you make small investments over time. If you wait until you think you can afford it, it could be too late. For example, a woman told me that in 30 years of marriage, she and her husband only went on two vacations alone together. In the early years of their marriage, they created an elaborate plan to save money every month so they would have a significant nest egg when it was time to retire. Not a bad thing to do, but not if a plan controls your life and harms relationships. If putting a certain amount of money away each month (and not touching it) is always more important than spending money on date nights, romantic weekends, anniversary trips, or couples' retreats, something needs to be adjusted. Now that their kids are out of the nest and her husband has retired, they have their nest egg all right, but their relationship is cracking.

7. *Definition of a bargain.* I grew up wearing nice clothes because my mother owned dress shops and her daughters were walking advertisements for her business. In addition to inheriting her taste, I learned that well-made garments, though more expensive, usually last longer. It took me a

FROM THE HEART

You know the old saying, "He who has the most toys wins"? Don't believe it. He who has the best relationships wins. You'll never meet a person who looks back on life and says, "I should have created a larger company" or "I should have created more wealth by working longer hours."

SMART MOVE

Small savings add up to big rewards.

- The average cost of car insurance in the United States is about $850 per year. If your car insurance deductible is $500, raising it to $1,000 can reduce premium costs by 40 percent (or about $340), according to the Insurance Information Institute.

- The average cost of a restaurant lunch is almost $10. Bringing lunch from home a couple of days a week can mean a potential savings of $1,000 a year.

- If you don't use the allotted minutes in your cell phone plan, look for a plan with fewer minutes. It may cost less. If you use too many minutes each month, raise the limit. It's cheaper than paying the overage fees.

while to convince Bill that one well-made suit was better than several bargain versions.

8. *No "yours" and "mine."* Marriage is a total commitment of all you are and have to each other. Holding on to "your" money sends a clear signal that you're not fully committed to the relationship and often leads to separate lives and little accountability. If you decide to have separate checking accounts, do so with an attitude of openness and answerability.

9. *Enjoying God's blessings.* Although the Bible outlines a number of uses for money, one purpose is for the enjoyment of God's blessings. Wealth isn't meant for our wasteful indulgence, but God "richly gives us all we need for our enjoyment" (1 Timothy 6:17).

10. *Contentment.* None of us always gets what we want or think we deserve. Welcome to life. Sometimes we get more, sometimes less, but most of the time we have more than we need. The goal is contentment.

Life is predictably unpredictable. Every one of our children had birth complications; each birth drained our resources. Years later unexpected business circumstances threw us into new financial peril. A few years after that, my four breast cancer surgeries set off insurance company fireworks. With each crisis, as the Family Manager, I had to ask myself hard questions.

Would I let tough times make me bitter or better?
During a crisis, what would be the tone in our home?

If something positive was to come from difficult situations, I knew that to a large extent, the possibility rose or fell with my attitude. As a family, we resolved to pull together and keep our collective attitude creatively and consciously focused on our blessings. Scanning past the things we couldn't do, we fixed our gaze on the long list of things we *could* do—many of them free or low cost. As it turns out, three of life's greatest gifts bear neither price tag nor bar code: laughter, music, and nature—all are free. So what if we couldn't take the entire family to a traveling Broadway play on opening night? We could rent a video, pop popcorn, and prop our feet on the coffee table. For that matter, we could catch a matinee.

Now that you know our family's fiscal policy, I urge you and your spouse to begin working to articulate your own. Make separate lists of what you each think matters and then look for the items that overlap—that shared real estate in the Venn diagram of the things you both value. When you're finished, you'll feel new energy from information, insights, and ideas that may not have occurred to either of you at the start.

low-cost family fun

Building bonds with your spouse and kids will benefit everyone. The good news: finding shared activities doesn't need to consume great amounts of money, time, or energy. Perhaps you and your family can try one of the activities listed below later today—or maybe it will spark another idea better suited to your family.

Spring

- Get outside. On a warm but windy day, head to the nearest open space with kites and a picnic. Or play a family game of H-O-R-S-E at a nearby school's outdoor basketball court.
- Play disc golf. Make a disc golf course in your backyard. Draw large numbers on paper plates and attach them to things—trees, shrubs, fences—to designate each "hole," which each player must hit with a Frisbee.
- Watch the stars. Lie on a blanket in the backyard with an astronomy chart and a flashlight.

Summer

- Check your community calendar. Many cities and towns sponsor fairs, festivals, outdoor concerts, classic car shows, or farmers markets during the summer. Most are free or low cost. Check your town's Web site or newsletter for details.
- Look at your backyard with new eyes. If you live in a house, could you plant a garden or build a tree house together? If you are in an apartment, maybe you could hang bird feeders on the shrubs outside your patio or put flower boxes along your balcony. The whole family can be involved in such projects.
- Have a family car wash. Wear bathing suits and be ready for sponge fights and water-hose wars.

GOOD TO KNOW

Americans are paring down the list of appliances they can't live without, according to a 2009 Pew Research Center survey. About half now see a microwave oven, a TV set, and air-conditioning as luxuries rather than necessities.

SMART MOVE

Use a debit card. You'll have a record of every purchase you make, it's easy to track expenses, and you won't have to carry around a lot of cash.

Fall

- Go on a scavenger hunt at a zoo. Check online and make a list of the animals you will see. Have your child try to locate each animal on the list.
- Go on an animal safari. One night, take turns hiding stuffed animals around your house. Have other family members form teams, then turn off all the lights and use a flashlight to go on a safari to capture the animals. After four or five minutes, see which team has captured the most.
- Invent a new flavor of ice cream. Begin with a plain flavor and add nuts, chocolate chips, crumbled candy bars, crushed cookies, chocolate-coated candies, or peanut butter. Brainstorm together about what you'll call it.

Winter

- Let it snow. If you live in the right climate, celebrate the first significant snowfall by sledding or engaging in a family snowball fight.
- A day at the museum. Many galleries and museums offer free admission on certain days or at certain times each week. Use these opportunities to learn and experience new things together.
- Start an ongoing tournament. Get out your favorite board game and have a weekend tournament, tallying each person's score for the game. Award a small prize to the overall winner.

seven financial mistakes to avoid

As you begin formulating your family's financial strategy, I encourage you to be aware of a number of common, yet avoidable, financial missteps.

1. *Don't fail to track cash.* If halfway through the month you're already puzzled about how you're going to make it until the end of the month and even more puzzled over where the money has gone, you've got a problem—and the sooner you solve it, the better. Here's a suggestion: Estimate all the cash you'll need for the next week or two, and make one—and only one—trip to the ATM. Store the cash in an envelope in a secure place. Keep a pen handy to jot down how much

QUICK FIX

QUESTION: *My husband and I are having trouble paying our credit card debt. What one thing can we start doing today to reduce our debt?*

ANSWER: Negotiate with your creditors when you can't keep up with your bills. Be honest and explain your situation. They may allow you more time to pay, drop late fees, or even settle for less than the full amount you owe. Creditors would rather settle for less than spend money trying to collect and possibly get nothing. The downside is that negotiating your debts can dent your credit report. Also, if a lender does reduce a debt, the amount reduced is categorized as income and you may have to pay income tax on that amount.

GOOD TO KNOW

According to the Pew Research Center, 45 percent of women say they hold the family purse strings, compared to 37 percent of men who say they do.

and when you or your family members take out cash so you can track spending. You may find you're spending a lot more money than you thought on nonessentials.

Or you might try what one friend calls her "envelope method." At the first of the month, she withdraws the cash she needs to pay for her family's household expenses (not bills) for a month. She puts budgeted amounts for specific categories in labeled envelopes—groceries, drugstore items, entertainment, school supplies, clothing, babysitting, miscellaneous—and keeps them in a drawer. She pays cash for everything, and when the money is gone for the month, it's gone.

2. *Don't enable a clueless spouse.* I've known several women whose husbands never told them anything about their finances. And frankly, they didn't care to know as long as their monthly "allowance" showed up and they could spend it any way they liked. When one friend's husband died suddenly at age 50, she didn't have a clue about their assets, liabilities, insurance, or other financial matters—which added a lot of unnecessary stress to her already painful situation. A woman I met recently at a conference told me that her marriage is

crumbling because she manages all the family finances and her husband takes little interest in knowing how much money is in the bank or when the bills get paid.

Most couples fall someplace between these two extremes. What's important is that you both know what you own, where to locate important records and documents, and who's going to pay which bills. In our family, we decided to split up financial management. Bill pays the mortgage, insurance, utilities, and all monthly expenses out of one account. I opened a special household checking account to pay for groceries, clothing, haircuts, school needs, and the like. And because I wanted to make sure we had a little extra to create memories on family trips, I tucked away dollars so I could surprise the family with a day of river rafting or horseback riding.

3. *Don't fail to plan, save, and give.* Unless you have a plan to limit spending, you and your spouse are likely to spend more than you make. Every family needs a saving and giving plan. The best way to do this is to take out any amounts you want to save and give as soon as you are paid. This forces you to limit spending. Automatic payroll deductions are a good way to do this. Financial experts suggest that you have six months' worth of living expenses in a readily accessible interest-bearing account. Those who are self-employed or work in a high turnover industry should have up to a year's worth of living expenses tucked away.

   Use the Finding Ways to Save worksheet on page 123 to brainstorm ways you can work as a family to cut costs. You may be surprised at the money you can save. You might even discover that the downturn improves the quality of your relationships as you work together.

4. *Don't overuse credit cards.* Credit cards are a wonderful convenience and a terrible temptation. It's just so much easier to pull out the credit card to make an impulse buy than to pay cash. It doesn't seem like real money. But actually, it's real money plus interest (if you don't pay it off right away). There's no better way to perpetuate debt—or waste your money—than to carry a credit card balance. Items bought on credit and carried on a card over months can cost much more than you would have ever considered spending with cash. That really cute purse on sale for 20 percent off can end up

Finding Ways to Save

CATEGORY	GOAL	IDEA	ANTICIPATED SAVINGS
Example: **Electricity**	*Reduce electric bill*	*Install automatic thermostat*	*$11/mo.*
Housing			
Utilities			
Food			
Transportation			
Clothing			
Entertainment			
Insurance			
Taxes			
Vacations			
Holidays/Gifts			
Health/Medical			

costing you 120 percent. Making only the minimum monthly payments will cost you thousands in interest fees that could otherwise be applied toward savings or a family vacation.

Also, don't use more than one-third of your credit card's limit. Having a higher balance reflects poorly on your credit report, even if you keep current with your payments.

5. *Don't assume bills and bank statements are correct.* We learned the hard way that companies and their computers make mistakes. Sure, errors are the exception and it's a pain to study the details, but when you discover a mistake six months after the fact, it's immeasurably more difficult to sort out and correct the problem. If you see something that doesn't look right, call and inquire—now.

Last year our son ran across several charges on his company credit card that looked strange. He called and at length discovered that someone had hacked into an office supply store's database and stolen his card information (along with the PIN the business was not supposed to store). He was finally able to sort out the fraud and get a reimbursement, but it took hours of his time and energy.

If you foresee a major medical claim in your future, get ready. When I battled breast cancer in 2007, scrutinizing bills and EOBs (explanation of benefits) became Bill's part-time job. One problem was that the hospital and physicians' offices sometimes failed to file proper claim reports, and because of that the insurance company failed to pay them. Another issue was that the insurance company was routinely denying legitimate claims. We had to stand our ground and fight for the hospital and physicians to be paid. Certainly, sometimes insurance companies make legitimate mistakes, but given our experience, my suggestion is to never assume charges are correct until you check your policy and confirm and then reconfirm your coverage.

6. *Don't cut out fun stuff.* When finances get really tight, it's tempting to let survival mode rob your family of the joys of life. Even if you're in the midst of a severe family bailout plan, if you eliminate fun and recreation altogether, your best-laid plans will eventually self-destruct. Okay, so summer passes to the theme park and dining out weekly have been the casualties of a line-item veto on the family budget, but you

Fun Family Outings for Less

For our three boys, a trip to Six Flags or a water park often launched our summers. Though getting a family of five in the gates without draining our bank account was a challenge, planning ahead made it possible. Some of the following tips may help you cut costs without cutting the fun—whether you're headed to a water park or any other park that charges admission.

Shop for discount coupons. Comb the Internet for coupons and check the Web sites of parks in your area; many parks offer Internet-only specials. Also look around for deals at local grocery stores, fast-food restaurants, and drugstores.

Consider attendance dates. Parks are busiest on weekends, so sometimes you can get better deals on weekdays. If you live near a park and plan to attend more than once this summer, check into season passes. They often pay for themselves by the second visit.

Arrive later and stay longer. Some parks offer a 20 to 50 percent discount for late arrivals, at 4 p.m. or after. (Check with the park for the specific time they offer twilight discounts.) You can still enjoy five to seven hours of fun before the park closes.

Pack your own food and drinks. Meals inside parks are pricey and often have little nutritional value. Check out the park's policies to find out whether you can bring in food. If you can, bring snacks and water bottles from home in a backpack that family members can take turns toting.

If outside food is not allowed in, you can plan a tailgate picnic in the parking lot. A friend in New Jersey says she arrives 30 minutes before the gates open so she can park close to the entrance. She keeps sandwiches, fruit, cold drinks, and bottles of water in a cooler so her crew of six can make quick trips back to the car for sustenance during the day.

Bring your own rafts, sports equipment, or other toys so you won't have to rent them. Bring some self-adhesive patches so you can repair punctured inflatable toys on the spot.

CAUTION!

Without realizing it, many parents in all income brackets ignore the law of diminishing returns—the more you get, the more you need to be satisfied—to their children's peril. In the case of parenting, it goes something like this: You buy a three-year-old an inexpensive toy, which pleases and occupies him for a while, but then he becomes bored and asks you to buy a new toy. So you buy him a little bigger and more costly toy, which may please him a little longer, but soon it, too, becomes old. Simply put: your child will continue to want more and more if you continue to buy him more and more.

still need to make room for fun. Scale back and determine to enjoy the best things in life. They're free, you know.

7. *Don't give kids too much.* We have three wonderful, well-adjusted sons who, from an early age and by the grace of God, understood that there were limits on what they could have. However, children come into this world wanting as much as they can have, and they don't want to be accountable

GOOD TO KNOW

For almost six in ten Americans, talking to kids about money increases family anxiety, while nearly 28 percent say it reduces it, according to a 2009 Marist Poll.

for what they do get. It's the human condition, which we all inherited from our original ancestors.

A wise friend related a story to us early in our parenting career that had a significant impact on the ways we raised our boys. Here's the sad real-life story. A boy growing up in an affluent part of town was given everything he wanted as a child—the newest toys, the best camps, the finest clothes. On his 16th birthday he was given an expensive (and fast) new car, along with his own checking account and a monthly allowance. Knowing no previous limits, he quickly accrued several speeding tickets and regularly overdrew his bank account—which his dad always covered without consequence. This pattern continued into adulthood, when his parents finally decided it had to stop, and they sought counsel from my friend who advised them to stop covering the checks. They didn't follow his advice, and their son eventually went to prison. No one forced him into behaving irresponsibly, but his parents unintentionally trained him to be this way.

Children must be taught that the privilege of having money brings great responsibility. Covering for them when they behave irresponsibly or replacing things they lose or don't maintain trains them to be irresponsible adults. Responsibility is like the measles: it's less painful when you get it as a child.

Never do anything or buy anything on a regular basis for your children that they are capable of doing or buying for themselves. Your job is to help them become independent, self-sufficient adults.

a man's point of view

managing finances

There's a story—maybe it's mythical—that during World War II, Winston Churchill looked out to sea and told an aide that the British needed to surface all the German subs. How? "Boil the ocean," Churchill said. The aide saluted the idea in so many words and then asked Churchill how he proposed to boil the ocean. Churchill replied, "I come up with the concepts. You work out the details."

This chapter about managing the Finances department in your home is a little like Churchill's instructions to his aide. We can give you the concepts, but every couple, every family, must work out their own details and live it for themselves. Not easy, but very important.

The Finances department has been voted most likely to divide—or at least fray nerves, tie stomachs in knots, and ruin a good night's sleep. And it's not a modern problem. Sometimes I wonder if the apostle Paul mediated household budget arguments since he wrote about the love of money being the root of all kinds of evil. In my grandparents' day, the man made the money and decided how it would be spent. In my parents' day, the man made the money and the woman spent it. Today, many dual-income couples categorize their money: yours, mine, and ours. None of these approaches provides a good paradigm for peaceful management of a family's Finances department. The good news, however, is that money has as much power to unite as it does to divide.

For young couples especially, working through personal values and merging two perspectives of what's financially "normal" can seem like navigating a bumper car ride: there are repeated slams as you cross someone else's path. Once again, the case study I know best is our own. And I'm here to say, the ride can be really bumpy.

The summer before our senior year of college, Kathy and I tied the knot, and our first year together was pretty effortless. Why wouldn't it be? Her mom and dad covered her tuition and continued her monthly allowance. And with my financial-aid package, you might say that our living on love was made possible by several grants.

Then came graduation and the official cutting of the apron strings. That's when I began to comprehend that "for richer or poorer" meant something different to Kathy than it did to me. Actually, she had no perception of poorer, and I had no perception of richer. My tightfisted approach to finances didn't mesh well with Kathy's there's-always-money-in-the-bank history. Both of us desperately

SMART MOVE

Buck the trend. Don't be like those people who spend their health seeking wealth in the first half of life and then must spend their wealth seeking health in the second half of life.

needed to create the new normal for our new family. After enduring numerous painful and unhelpful discussions, we finally stumbled upon healthier ways of sharing our desires and beliefs about money. As better communication created trust, we loosened our death grips on our inherited definitions of normal. Issue by issue, we began to exchange "what my parents always did" for "what we do."

 HIGHLY RECOMMENDED

No matter what your backgrounds, what's *yours* and what's *hers*, your way and her way must give way to finding common ground and crafting a family financial policy that's *ours*, something you both can live with. Completing the His Normal–Her Normal exercise on page 129 is a great way to start.

Don't underestimate what your spouse has to teach you. In *Defending the Caveman*—the one-man Broadway show about the gender gap—Rob Becker urges men and women to visit one another's world without judgment. When I began to do this, I found out that I had a lot to learn from Kathy—like the wisdom of buying a $150 pair of quality shoes that lasted five years as opposed to buying a $50 pair that wore out in a year. Kathy learned that she needed to keep up with the checks she wrote lest she run up overdraft charges that her mom wasn't around to cover.

Start by making your own list of what you've learned from your wife and what you would like for her to learn from you. Invite her to do the same—list what she has learned from you and what she would like you to learn from her. Then sit down with your wife and compare lists. Where do you find common ground? Decide what you can agree on together. From there, write down specific guidelines and financial principles you want to be part of your *new* family financial policy. (Kathy offered some of the keys of our own financial policy as a model. See pages 116–118.)

HIS NORMAL—HER NORMAL

finances

Consider the conflicts between you and your spouse that stem from the different ways your families managed finances when you were growing up. Discuss assumptions that you both brought into your marriage about "normal" ways couples deal with money issues. Listen and learn from each other; then negotiate your way to the "new normal" for your relationship. (See examples below.)

His Normal	**Our New Normal**	**Her Normal**
There were a lot of arguments about money in my house, usually about how much money my mother was spending on this or that. I'm anxious a lot when I don't know where our money is going.	We will not have "your" money and "my" money; however, we will keep two accounts, to which we'll both have access. We will discuss any purchase over $100, but we won't micromanage each other.	My parents both worked outside the home and had their own money. Mom took care of some expenses; Dad took care of others. Since I'm earning an income, I should be able to spend it the way I want to without discussion.
His Normal	**Our New Normal**	**Her Normal**

TECH TIP

There's a
useful tool at
www.jobsformoms
.com/income-test
to help you calculate
the cost of working
outside the home.

counting the cost of going back to work

As economic forecasts remain stormy, many families continue to struggle with reduced wages, increased expenses, and the threat of more layoffs. No one's got it easy, but one-income households are really feeling the pressure, pushing couples to consider sending Mom back into the workforce.

If finances are driving you to consider a job outside the home, be sure the payoff is worth the switch. Big expenses like child care and commuting costs can consume a sizable chunk of your paycheck. Small expenses (often overlooked) shrink it even more. For example, you'll probably need new work clothes and accessories, and even if you buy clothes that don't require dry cleaning, at times you may need some things cleaned and pressed. You may vow to take your lunch to work and prepare home-cooked meals, but with both parents working, eating out more is highly likely. And don't forget that additional income could push you into the next tax bracket.

Chad and Lindsey Sewell of Seattle say that when they married, they were not planning on having children. When Lindsey became pregnant, they wondered if it would be financially feasible for her to stay home with the baby. For two weeks they scrutinized their budget, looking for ways to get variable monthly expenses as fixed as possible. Chad says that after researching and a lot of number crunching and praying, they decided that Lindsey should quit her job as a travel agent to be a stay-at-home mom.

Today, Chad and Lindsey are the proud parents of five boys; frugality makes it possible for their household of seven to live on one paycheck. They admit it isn't always easy but say the benefits far outweigh the struggles. They know they made the right decision for their family.

When L.L. and Ka Cotter moved to Dallas in the 1970s with their young family, they decided that Ka would reenter the workforce. L.L. would adjust his schedule to handle more on the home front since Ka's job often required travel. Year after year, as Ka was promoted through the ranks, eventually to vice chairman of the Staubach Company, she and L.L. worked as a team to manage their home and rear their two children. Now their children have children of their own, and the Cotters are still a family team. Their solution proved to be a good one for their family.

If you are considering various jobs and the cost of going back to work, take a good look at the numbers and make sure that taking a certain position—or going back to work at all—is a financially sound idea. Consider job hunting at companies that offer positions with flexibility—condensed workweeks, part-time work, contract work, or jobs that allow some telecommuting—as this can cut your expenses. According to a new study from the Families and Work Institute, 94 percent of employers are maintaining or increasing workplace flexibility options during the recession.

If you're wondering if a job with flexibility could work for you, or before you try selling the idea of a flexible schedule to a current or potential employer, consider these questions:

1. Are you self-directed and do you work well independently?
2. Realistically, can your job be done away from an office environment? Does it require uninterrupted concentration, a lot of space, or special equipment? Can your job be done using a computer, e-mail, a fax machine, a pager, and/or voice mail? Will the company provide those? If not, can you cover the costs?
3. Would a compressed workweek—three 12-hour days or four 10-hour days—work as well or better than a typical nine-to-five schedule?
4. How will your boss supervise you? How often will you need to attend meetings at the office? Can he or she evaluate your work if you work at home?
5. What benefits can you sell to your employer? Increased flexibility to meet client and corporate needs—meaning special projects can be done after regular work hours? Reduced need for office space and parking? Fewer days off work (a sick child no longer means missed hours)? Increased employee satisfaction? Money saved by a reduction in your hours? Make your case on how the company will gain from the arrangement as well.

hanging together in tough times

These are difficult times for many families. As I finish writing this book, times are tough and financial forecasts are glum. Many people are preparing for what could be a prolonged economic

GOOD TO KNOW

American families today are working 539 hours more per year than families in 1970, reports the federal Bureau of Labor Statistics. This is an additional 13.5 weeks of full-time work.

GOOD TO KNOW

Self-employed men and women are significantly more satisfied with their jobs than other workers and have virtually the same family incomes as other workers. However, they feel more financial stress, according to a 2009 Pew Research Center survey.

QUICK FIX

QUESTION: *How can we encourage our teenagers to save money?*

ANSWER: Consider matching every dollar they save toward a major purchase like a car or college savings. If they have a job, you might suggest that they save a certain fixed percent of each paycheck. Direct deposit is the easiest way to make sure this happens. When they get a raise, suggest that instead of increasing their spending they save one-half of every raise they get. A friend told me that she started this practice when she was in her teens and now, in her 40s, she is quite wealthy. It's a good habit to adopt.

storm. Although tight finances are no fun, many couples say the upside to the financial downturn is the opportunity to change spending routines that have gotten out of hand and focus on the truly important things of life—family, faith, and friends.

Numerous moms across the country have told me they're taking the challenge head-on—making sacrifices and implementing cost-saving strategies. Instead of finding joy in splurging, they're finding joy in frugality and are getting creative about stretching resources.

Remember Ashley Nuzzo, the champion coupon clipper I introduced to you in chapter 4? She's a great example of how to thrive despite a smaller income. But she's far from the only resourceful woman out there.

One mom told me that she and her friends are taking clothing to resale shops hoping to recoup some of the cost of clothes from their bulging closets. She confessed (and wants to remain anonymous): "I'm recovering from my shopping-as-therapy habit." Not a bad place to start.

Angie Beller, a Dallas mother of four, has always watched for ways to stretch dollars, but recently she surprised even herself when she ended up "making" money on her child's birthday party (and if you're thinking she sold admission tickets, you're wrong). Here's how she did it: instead of paying $200 to rent a giant backyard inflatable for kids to bounce around in, Angie bought one on eBay. After the party, she neatly repackaged it, put it back up for sale on eBay as "only used once," and sold it for more than she paid

Moms for Hire

As the economy continues to drag, a lot of moms I know are creating their own family bailout plans by launching home-based businesses. If you're looking to join the ranks of the "momtrepreneurs"—moms who work from home while taking care of their families—your first step is to consider what kind of business would fit you best.

Don't overlook the obvious—if you once worked as an accountant, launching a part-time bookkeeping service makes sense—or the not-so-obvious. Consider the example of former kindergarten teacher Ellen Delap. After creating effective ways to organize time, space, supplies, and equipment in her classroom, she transferred those strategies and her love for teaching to a home-based organizing business in Houston.

Beyond career history, often the best entrepreneurial endeavors are spawned from a hobby a woman loves or a solution she created to meet a need in her own life—which may be a need other people have as well.

- Former journalist Susan Elliott of Dallas loves to cook, so she created a summer cooking camp for kids, which includes cooking lessons, fun crafts, and activities. The camp was a huge hit, so she self-published a book to show other moms how to start their own home-based summer camp built around their affinities—such as cheerleading, jewelry making, sewing, or painting.

- Christy Lafferty, a Dallas mother of two preschoolers, meshed her photography hobby with her love for babies and launched a home-based photography business.

- Veteran moms Kimberly Hope and Terri Haarala related to the younger moms in their neighborhood in Frisco, Texas, who wanted extra privacy while nursing their babies on the go. They created and marketed a nursing blanket that stays put on a mother's shoulder.

- Another mom in Frisco, Amy Richmond, created beautiful but inexpensive jewelry for herself and her daughter and ended up turning the idea into a whole line of jewelry and gifts that focus on the blessing of motherhood.

TECH TIP

Sell and buy gently used children's toys at www.kidzola.com.

SMART MOVE

Working from home requires an extra dose of discipline and organization to blend your paying and caregiving jobs successfully. Schedule specific blocks of time for chores, errands, exercise, time with friends, and so on. Designate specific blocks to give your children your full, undivided attention (i.e., turn off all electronic devices).

for it. The difference covered the cost of decorations, party favors, and food. She even had a little money left over.

Autumn Thomson of Tallahassee threw a pajama party for her three-year-old daughter at Krispy Kreme. She bought small pillows at a dollar store for a pillow fight and bought all the guests doughnuts and milk—plus coffee for parents. They hosted about 25 kids and about 30 parents, and spent less than $75 total.

Regardless of the type of party, if you plan in advance, get input from your child, and keep the guest list to a manageable size, you can throw a successful party and maintain your budget in the process. Plus, you can add free treats to the day by signing up your child at www.FreeBirthdayTreats.com.

Melissa Tarun, mother of two from Helotes, Texas, told me of her plan to painlessly cut $1,785 from her family's annual budget. Her ideas included:

- Cancel seven magazine subscriptions: save $84.
- Cancel unlimited-access movie rental plan: save $156.
- Melissa and her two girls will get fewer haircuts, and Melissa will try to cut back on highlighting sessions for an expected savings of $452.
- Her second grader takes her lunch to school almost every day, and Melissa follows a zero-waste policy while packing her lunches—no paper napkins, juice boxes, or plastic bags. Expected savings (compared to buying school lunches and disposable products for packed lunches): $277.

surviving and thriving through the really tough times

Of course, many families are facing more difficult sacrifices and making serious lifestyle changes. A number of women have told me stories of having to move out of their foreclosed homes. Many have lost their jobs. I can tell you firsthand that it is emotionally draining and even frightening to do battle with health insurance giants that find ways not to pay what you understood was included in your coverage.

When we're walking through difficult life passages, we have four possible responses:

Don't Forfeit the Joy of Giving

Live out your philosophy of giving by practicing hospitality and volunteering as a family in your community. This is a memorable way to teach kids the importance of giving to others. A recent survey revealed that more than a third of American households make volunteering together a part of family life.

- Brainstorm as a family how you might serve others. You might like to do something to help older people in your neighborhood, work with a church youth program, volunteer at community sports events, or participate in an environmental program.
- Check out how your family might help serve a meal at a local homeless shelter.
- Work together as a family and host a "new kid on the block" party for a new neighbor. Make it a potluck, and have other neighbors exchange names and phone numbers with the newcomers. Put together a welcome packet; include a homemade map of the immediate neighborhood, phone numbers for services and community resources, and brochures from the library, museum, and zoo.
- Select a worthy charity or mission to support as a family. Have a garage sale and donate the profits.
- Spend part of your vacation going on a mission trip as a family.

FROM THE HEART

Ask yourself how much is enough. Unbridled wants fuel discontentment and drive us to work harder—often at the expense of relationships that are much more valuable.

1. We can blame others.
2. We can blame ourselves.
3. We can blame God.
4. Or we can make the best of the situation.

While we can't always control what happens to us, we can choose how to react to it. We can always choose to give thanks for what we *do* have rather than complain about what we *don't* have. We can always choose to focus on what we *can* do instead of what we *can't* do. And if we don't? We fall into the "if only" trap—and it's deadly. "If only I had _____ or _____, then I'd be happy." We focus on our liabilities, some of which are real—but greatly blown out of proportion—and some of which are imagined. We lose perspective, spew bitter words, and make rash decisions—creating a miserable journey for ourselves and those around us. It doesn't have to be this way.

When I find myself overly anxious or fearful about financial issues, I remind myself of the people who were working on the top floors of the World Trade Center buildings on September 11, 2001. When the two planes transected the buildings and people realized there was no hope for their rescue, did they call and yell at their spouse about a credit card bill? Or lash out at their financial planner because their interest income dropped last month? No, story after story told by the victims' family members reveal that they called to tell them of their love, to apologize, and to ask forgiveness for past hurts. In a few seconds their perception of what was most important in life became crystal clear.

working through financial hardship

In the late 1990s, our family experienced a financial meltdown. I made an impulsive business decision to bring on business partners with different values than ours, which resulted in 18 months of legal battles that drained our savings and our emotions. The whole situation was fraught with the potential to destroy our marriage, but instead our relationship grew stronger. There are at least six reasons why.

1. *We didn't point fingers and blame.* I knew I had exercised bad judgment and made serious mistakes, but when Bill acknowledged that he had not spoken up when he knew I was headed down a dangerous path, it allowed us both to deal with our poor choices honestly.
2. *We forgave each other.* Mistakes are hard to admit if you feel battered with judgment and condemnation. Knowing your own need for grace makes you want to extend grace to each other.
3. *We let go of grudges.* We believed that resentment would harm us personally, harm our relationship, and harm our ability to move positively into the future. We had friends who had suffered financial setbacks, and they never recovered because both the husband and the wife refused to forgive each other. Resentment keeps you looking back, focused on the past rather than on what you can change in the future. Letting go of resentment and forgiving enables you to look for solutions.

4. *We reminded each other that every experience can be redemptive.* Pain is a powerful teacher; it seems there are just some things we can't learn—or won't learn—unless we fail. To learn and grow from our mistakes, honest, soul-searching evaluation is important. Even if your current situation was caused by external forces such as a job layoff, God can redeem the situation for good.

5. *We prayed daily.* Somewhere along the way we had forgotten that God is our provider. We had also stopped praying together. Small wonder our financial ship ran aground. Today, we are both thankful for this wake-up call. Every night when we go to bed, we thank God for His provision for the day and for allowing us to do our work for Him. We thank Him that He is at work during the night not only protecting us while we rest but continuing His work. And we thank Him that when we awaken, we can join Him again.

6. *We didn't dwell on failure or wallow in guilt.* Magnifying failure is debilitating. Not being willing to forgive yourself or accept God's forgiveness will erode the confidence and courage you need to take reasonable risks and can paralyze your ability to make decisions.

No matter how hard the financial downturn has hit your family, now is a good time to assess your relationship with money, because it can build or destroy relationships that are infinitely more valuable. If you're just starting married life, serious thinking about your financial goals and philosophy now will pay long-term dividends you can't begin to estimate. If you're well into the journey—even if your kids are grown and gone—it's never too late to fine-tune your strategy. The ACT worksheets, which begin on page 139, are a great tool as you begin outlining your own financial priorities and strategy.

FROM THE HEART

Before marriage we think in terms of better, richer, and in good health. The key to marriage is knowing how to walk together through the worse times, financial downturns, and serious illness.

THE MOST IMPORTANT THINGS TO REMEMBER

1. Before marriage couples think in terms of better, richer, and in good health. The key to marriage is knowing how to walk through worse times, financial downturns, and serious illness.

2. Every family needs a financial policy—the guardrails that keep you all on the same route going up the mountain.

3. Money has the power to destroy relationships, which are infinitely more valuable than your savings.

4. Everything you have belongs to God and is a gift from Him.

5. When you and your spouse encounter financial calamity, you'll weather the crisis better by walking through it together.

6. If you haven't decided what you value in life, you are more likely to feel insecure, discontented, and unable to enjoy the blessings you do have, especially when money is tight.

7. Three of life's greatest gifts bear neither price tag nor bar code: laughter, music, and nature—all are free.

8. No matter what the backgrounds of you and your spouse, what's *yours* and what's *mine*, your way and my way must give way to finding common ground and crafting a family financial policy that's *ours*—something everyone can live with.

9. What you leave *in* your children is far more important than what you leave *to* them.

10. Don't cover for your children when they behave irresponsibly with money or their belongings; this trains them to be irresponsible adults. Responsibility is like the measles: it's less painful when you get it as a child.

11. A financial downturn is the opportunity to change spending routines that have gotten out of hand and focus on the truly important things of life—family, faith, and friends.

12. If you strive after wealth at the expense of family life, personal health, and a healthy marriage, you will find that you really don't control your wealth—it controls you.

13. Managing money is not about the money. It's about how you view money.

finances department

Take a few minutes to think about the key causes of stress in the Finances department of your home. You and your spouse should use a different color pen or pencil to circle the number that best describes your individual stress level for each topic.

Key: 1=No Stress; 5=Very Stressful (0=Not Applicable)

Living according to what we value most	0	1	2	3	4	5
Bill paying	0	1	2	3	4	5
Monthly cash flow	0	1	2	3	4	5
Budgeting	0	1	2	3	4	5
Debt	0	1	2	3	4	5
Investments	0	1	2	3	4	5
Savings	0	1	2	3	4	5
Giving	0	1	2	3	4	5
Education costs	0	1	2	3	4	5
Retirement	0	1	2	3	4	5
ATM routine	0	1	2	3	4	5
Late fees/overdraft fees	0	1	2	3	4	5
Legal issues	0	1	2	3	4	5
Credit issues	0	1	2	3	4	5
Alimony/child-support issues	0	1	2	3	4	5
Tax returns	0	1	2	3	4	5
Receipts/records	0	1	2	3	4	5
Filing system	0	1	2	3	4	5
Kids' financial expectations	0	1	2	3	4	5
Kids' allowances	0	1	2	3	4	5
Shopping	0	1	2	3	4	5
Returns/store credits	0	1	2	3	4	5
Home office operations	0	1	2	3	4	5
Care for extended family members	0	1	2	3	4	5
Other _____	0	1	2	3	4	5
Other _____	0	1	2	3	4	5
Other _____	0	1	2	3	4	5
Other _____	0	1	2	3	4	5
Other _____	0	1	2	3	4	5
Other _____	0	1	2	3	4	5

finances department

Your Priorities

Look again at the items in the previous chart that you ranked as a 4 or a 5. Then you and your spouse should read the "I want" statements below and place a check in the box next to the ones that best describe your priorities for managing the Finances department in your home. Circle two or three that you each deem most important.

I want ...

his	hers	
❑	❑	to share financial goals with my spouse.
❑	❑	to spend our money according to what's most important to us.
❑	❑	to create a lifestyle we can sustain, live within our budget, and spend less than we make.
❑	❑	to become accountable as a couple for what we spend.
❑	❑	to divide financial tasks with my spouse and rotate responsibilities as we deem appropriate.
❑	❑	to pay our bills on time.
❑	❑	to pay off our credit card debt.
❑	❑	to be a good steward of our money and resources.
❑	❑	to teach our children that we are not what we own, wear, or drive, and that each of us is a valuable, unique human being.
❑	❑	to be thankful for what we have.
❑	❑	to be generous with our resources.
❑	❑	to stop buying things we really don't need.
❑	❑	to teach our children a healthy respect for money.
❑	❑	to be alert for little ways to save money here and there.
❑	❑	to invest money in things that strengthen our marriage.
❑	❑	to invest money in things that make positive memories for our family.
❑	❑	to save money for something we dream of.
❑	❑	to create a simple way to organize our important financial information.
❑	❑	to enroll in a financial management course offered by a church or organization.
❑	❑	_____
❑	❑	_____
❑	❑	_____

Your Goal

Consider your individual and shared priorities, then write an overall goal that reflects your desires for the Finances department. For this purpose, think of a goal as a broad, general, timeless statement that describes your overall aim for this department. Sometimes it is helpful to begin by identifying the key words that you'd use to describe this department when it runs well. Here's an example:

> **Key Words:** *save more, give more, cut expenses, budgeting*
>
> **Goal:** *To look for practical ways every day to reduce expenses so we can live within our budget; to increase the amounts we save and give away each month by at least 5 percent each.*

Key Words: _____

_____

Goal: _____

_____

finances department

Using this worksheet, divide up responsibilities for the Finances department.

Who's Responsible for What?

Responsibilities	Who does it now?	Who else could do it?
Establish/review financial priorities	_____	_____
Create budgets	_____	_____
Maintain records and file documents	_____	_____
Study bills for accuracy	_____	_____
Organize and pay bills	_____	_____
Prepare gifts for religious/charitable organizations	_____	_____
Create and store passwords and PINs	_____	_____
Pay household workers	_____	_____
Check bank statements for accuracy	_____	_____
Select appropriate charities	_____	_____
Work with a financial planner	_____	_____
Select appropriate investments/savings plans	_____	_____
Establish/maintain good credit	_____	_____
Research/buy insurance	_____	_____
File health insurance claims	_____	_____
Keep up with receipts	_____	_____
Deal with legal issues	_____	_____
Work with attorney to update wills	_____	_____
Process rebate forms	_____	_____
Collect/organize information for income taxes	_____	_____
Keep licenses and taxes paid	_____	_____
Identify ways to cut household spending	_____	_____
Shop for best deals on banking, mortgages, credit cards, and utilities	_____	_____
Keep home office supplies stocked	_____	_____
Get operating cash from bank/ATM	_____	_____
Disperse children's allowances	_____	_____
Other _____	_____	_____
Other _____	_____	_____
Other _____	_____	_____
Other _____	_____	_____

seven: managing special events

Twenty-five years from now, your kids' mental family scrapbooks will fall open, not to images of neatly stacked laundry piles or your fingerprint-free front door, but to memories of your annual family cookie-baking night in December and the time on vacation when you finally gave up your search for a McDonald's, only to stumble on an out-of-the-way ice cream parlor that served the most delicious homemade ice cream you've ever eaten.

Your kids likely won't remember the rainy Saturday you cleaned out the entire freezer. Instead they'll tell their kids about the scavenger hunt you arranged every Valentine's Day and the Fridays you celebrated report card upgrades with deep-dish pizza. When it comes to making memories, special occasions turn not on large amounts of money or talent but on grateful hearts, a boatload of flexibility, and life-sustaining humor.

who's your chief celebration officer?

Mom, most likely it is you who usually takes notes on this topic. But the idea is to get your husband more involved and to approach special events more as a team, so even *you* can enjoy them—and your family can enjoy a less-stressed you. All days, special or not, tend to rise and fall with Mom and her attitude.

Well, her attitude and some planning.

Parties, birthdays, graduations, new jobs, vacations, showers, weddings, anniversaries, Christmas, and other holidays all fall in the Special Events department of the Family Manager's job. Each

SMART MOVE

Every child's mind is a curator of memories. It's your privilege to paste pictures in mental scrapbooks, to wrap moments they'll open and reexamine years later. Talk with your spouse about how you want your children to remember your family's special events and occasions.

CAUTION!

We dream about making positive family memories when the kids get older, when we get a promotion, when we can buy a bigger, better house. When, when, when. Suddenly 20 years have gone by, allowing many important moments and memories to slip by. Don't let this happen in your family.

GOOD TO KNOW

Americans list a lack of money (61 percent), the pressures of gift giving (42 percent), lack of time (34 percent), and credit card debt (23 percent) as top causes of holiday stress, according to the American Psychological Association.

event, to varying degrees, asks us to think ahead, find information, perhaps delegate, meet intermittent deadlines, and follow through.

Stay with me on that last paragraph. Family occasions are as easy or involved as you want to make them. The single essential ingredient—we're back to that—is how you take it on.

If relationships within your family are strained, or if you are struggling to get overspending or an overflowing calendar under control, making plans to commemorate an upcoming special day or event may seem overwhelming. In fact, deleting it altogether may sound like a good solution. Ignoring special events, however, takes much of the joy and celebration out of life.

If you were raised in a home where holidays and celebrations were seen as extra expense and trouble, you may tend to go over-board to make up for festivities you missed as a child. Making a big deal of holidays and celebrations is not a bad thing, unless you make your family and everyone in the county miserable because everything about the celebration—the house, menu, decorations, table settings—has to be perfect.

Or maybe you feel pressured to outdo friends, outshine neighbors, or please your mother, who entertains lavishly. If so, impressing others with how you decorate, commemorate, and cele-brate can easily become more important than the meaning of the occasion or the people you're honoring. Or perhaps you and your husband are at odds because when you think special occasion, you think festive. But when he thinks special occasion, he thinks frivolous.

avoiding toxic extremes

Instead of going to one of these toxic extremes—skipping occa-sions outright or making the event so big that your stress hits the red level—I advocate lightening up and doing less. Scale back and adapt. Infinitely more important than no event or a perfect event are family relationships, traditions, and common experiences that link you to one another and to generations behind and before you. Tradi-tions and family occasions build your collective story and add to the pride of "who our family is." It's no small thing for a child to be able to say, "In my family, we always . . ."

Once again, it's important that you and your spouse determine what normal looks like in your household. Depending on your family makeup and which holidays and events make your crowd's collective heart leap, you may rise to a few or many occasions a year. Not every event necessitates a planning binder and weeks of work. Some spring up with short notice. But nothing gets you nothing, as they say. To fail to plan is to plan to fail.

To put that positively: envision the happy times, the memories to come, the family bonding that can take place with even a little advance thought! Remember the third time-management truth: You can plan, but you can't predict? The can't-miss Special Events

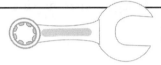

QUICK FIX

QUESTION: *My children are constantly bringing home requests from their schools asking for volunteers to serve as room moms, provide refreshments for fund-raisers, or chaperone on field trips. I work full-time and have children at two different schools. I want them to feel like I'm contributing to the special events at their schools but already feel overwhelmed.*

ANSWER: At the beginning of a school year or semester, tell your children to watch for one volunteer opportunity that they would like you to sign up for, such as driving on one field trip or working in the school cafeteria during lunch one day. If they really don't care that you are present for something, offer to send cookies or bars to a function. Bake them together the night before. Also, it's not just moms who volunteer these days. Talk to your husband about signing up for one volunteer opportunity too. An ideal volunteer situation would be one where both of you can serve at the same function where your child is present, like a fall carnival or the concession stand at a field day. Just don't let guilt push you into volunteering when those calls for help come home in your child's backpack. Be wise about what you choose and how much time it will take away from your home and family.

FROM THE HEART

Bill and I have found that when we pray together before a special event, God has a way of giving us the emotional buoyancy we need when things go wrong.

equation is Plans + Flexibility = Family Fun (F squared). Never did that basic equation apply more directly than now.

Yes, it's true that to set an agenda is human. To set an agenda and expect it to stay in stone, however, is a gold-embossed invitation to anxiety and disappointment. Do not, I repeat, do not build your family's special day on impressing your mother, your best friend, Martha Stewart, a visiting dignitary, the neighbor who makes her own pasta . . . or yourself. Build it on joy. Every year's best-impression award ultimately goes to the mother who has a "roll with it" mind-set, the life-giving mix of planning and humor. As my father advises, "Make the most with what you've got," which throws wide the double doors for everyone (including you) to delight in a special day as it comes, making what's most important, most important.

The object, as you recall, is positive memories, not pass-along recipes. $P + F = F^2$.

a man's point of view

managing special events

Do you ever wonder why your wife seems overly stressed in December? Do you two routinely argue the day you leave for vacation? If answers to these questions are a mystery to you, as they once were to me, I'm about to let you in on a secret that will make your life a lot more pleasant.

Don't blame her behavior on hormones or the stage of the moon. There's something else going on here: in the midst of her already busy life, she's managing a big project to create great family memories—often without your help.

Here's a personal illustration. Every year when our boys were young, we would load them in the car before dawn for a cross-country trip to Crested Butte, Colorado, for our family vacation. Before we were 10 miles down the road—without fail—Kathy and I were bickering. Why? Well, for weeks she had been planning the trip—figuring out logistics, arranging for the mail and paper to be stopped, preparing and packing the kids' clothing and gear, figuring out who would feed and care for the dog, planning en route snacks and menus, creating games and activities to occupy the kids during the trip, and checking in with friends we planned to meet on the way.

What did I do? Well, for the most part, I just showed up. I worked until the last minute, threw my clothes and fishing gear in the car, and jumped behind the wheel, eager and ready for a relaxing vacation. So I'm thinking everyone's happy . . . why shouldn't they be? We were heading out of the Texas heat and were on our way to the mountains.

Finally, after more years than I'd rather reveal, I'd had enough; so I asked Kathy, "What's wrong with you? This happens every year!" In reply I got an earful of frustration over my lack of helpfulness. When I asked Kathy to make a list of all the things that needed to be done before we left, I was shocked. Painful as the workout session was, it marked the end of our unpleasant vacation routine and the beginning of my understanding of the Special Events department.

Vacations, along with holidays, birthday parties, family celebrations, and other large and small events that require project management over and above routine daily duties fall into the Special Events department of the Family Manager system. This department includes all the family events—whether they're small or large, once-in-a-lifetime or annual celebrations—that fall outside the normal routine of daily activities. Birthdays, vacations, Christmas and other holidays, parties, weddings, anniversaries, and family reunions are all special projects. Things like building or remodeling a house, heading up a school or community fund-raiser, or orchestrating a garage sale also fall into the category of Special Events.

Each project in this department calls for planning, research, compilation of data, delegation, and meeting intermittent deadlines. Each project requires careful follow-through until it comes to a definite close—just like a work project.

Let's say you are part of a two-person team at work

TECH TIP

No need to wait until you get home to start sharing photos from birthdays, holidays, and other special occasions. AirMe is a cell phone application that allows you to upload photos instantly to Flickr, Photobucket, Picasa, TinyPic, Facebook, and Twitter.

SMART MOVE

After a holiday cele-
bration or special
event, no matter
what went wrong,
be sure to give
credit where credit
is due. Compliment
and thank family
members for their
effort—even if it's
for something they
did wrong but it
ended up as a funny
story in the family
joke bank. And give
yourself credit as
well. You've just
added a memory to
your family's legacy.

that is responsible for a big project. Let's also say that your partner picks up 5 percent of the responsibilities, leaving you to shoulder 95 percent of the tasks. On top of that, your partner doesn't know how many extra hours you've devoted to the project and how many sacrifices you've made to your normal routine. I imagine you'd be feeling some resentment and there'd be some friction in the office.

Now apply this scenario to your home and all the special-occasion projects your wife shoulders, and you'll have an idea of how she feels. Take the holiday season, for example. Christmas is particularly challenging because it's generally the biggest special event of the year. Like any successful project, all the holiday activities require planning, research and development, delegation, follow-through, and scheduled deadlines. With a little teamwork, the month of December can be an enjoyable, memorable time for the entire family, even the Family Manager!

What matters most about Special Events—whether we're talking about a family reunion, birthday party, Fourth of July picnic, or graduation celebration—are the reasons behind the events: honoring those we love, carrying on traditions, celebrating our faith, cementing family bonds, or just plain working together on a garage sale to generate some extra cash from the clutter we've cleared out of the attic.

Special Events are also important memory makers for our kids, whose minds are constantly recording information. Psychologists say it's the unusual or out-of-the-ordinary happenings—good and bad—that form our strongest memories. This means that our kids won't remember how many deals we closed or if the kitchen floor was mopped daily. But they will remember gathering with family friends for tailgate parties each autumn. They'll also remember the family reunion when you jumped through hoops to secure reservations at a "luxurious" campground, only to arrive and learn that the portable toilets didn't work. Times like these are crucial to a family's culture and cohesion.

It's traditions, holidays, and special family occasions—the times when we laugh, love, and enjoy life together—that bind a family together.

HIGHLIGHTED RECOMMENDED

HIGHLY RECOMMENDED

If arguments and unmet expectations have drowned out fun on your family's special days, now is a good time to decide to do things differently, to talk about how you can share the work and increase the joy for you both—and everyone else, for that matter. If your children are old enough, gather around a bowl of popcorn and ask them about their favorite family memories. Take note. What do they consider the most important holidays, seasons, and family happenings? What makes those times memorable?

Also carve out some time just with your wife. With pencil, paper, and calendar in hand, turn off the TV and talk about your normal, her normal, and your new normal. (See the His Normal–Her Normal worksheet on page 151.) Then use the What Will Your Children Remember? worksheet on page 152 as a jumping-off point to discuss which specific family traditions, holidays, and special occasions you want to be a part of your family's culture. Talk about what you can contribute and how you can work together so special events are enjoyable for everyone.

FROM THE HEART

Start a family gratitude book. Years ago we started recording things for which we were thankful after each Thanksgiving meal. It's fun to look back and see our entries from 20 years back. Add to your book after family vacations and celebrations too.

simple celebrations, treasured traditions

As noted before, not everyone grew up with treasured traditions or happy memories of family events. And not everyone has the celebration or party gene. For those of us not strong in the Menus and Meals department, special occasions can be particularly challenging because food is central to many holidays and celebrations. But anyone can begin today to make some days special.

Fix yourself a cup of tea, move everything off your favorite chair, and sit down with me a moment. Think about the happiest special occasions you've had so far as a couple or a family. Remember the disasters that, with time, you're already starting to laugh about. Remember the times you pulled off a memorable special event— and what you'd do differently now.

Then invite your spouse to sit in and tell him your ponderings. If you need to apologize for times when you've expected him to be

SMART MOVE

Don't expect perfect behavior from your kids before or during your special event. Anticipation often reaches an intense pitch, and kids often grow overly excited. Manage your response; deal with misbehavior calmly and in private. Agree as a couple to "watch each other's back." If one parent gets close to the boiling point, the other can bring perspective and patience to a situation.

a mind reader and know exactly what you wanted him to do, or if you spewed criticism because you thought his attempt at teamwork was subpar, start there. Ask for his forgiveness—even if you feel 90 percent of the problem was his. Taking care of your 10 percent will go a long way toward tearing down any walls of resentment that have built up over time.

Then discuss the ways you want to continue to give your family reasons to celebrate—and memories to return to. If you can love the process and laugh at the imperfections, your kids will learn, without a word from you, that special days merit special effort and special tolerance. It's worth your time—and it's fun, to boot—to honor what deserves honor, to observe family traditions, to work out the details together, and to see the final product sporting all your fingerprints.

Important note: you don't need to wait for a birthday, holiday, or life milestone to make positive memories. You can make any day a special occasion. One mom told me she was in the midst of a horrific week when her youngest daughter learned to blow a bubble. That evening she used the good china. After dinner, she served pieces of gum on a platter and the entire family blew bubbles together. You think her daughter remembers that?

a dozen ways to celebrate every day

Here are a dozen ways you can turn an ordinary day into a special memory or celebration.

1. Launch a family awards night. Give personalized awards for categories such as Fastest Dishwasher, Most Improved Laundry Folder, Grill King, or Sweet Potato Queen.
2. Make a big deal out of finishing a monumental task, such as putting up a basketball hoop or cleaning the house from top to bottom. Make a special dessert to enjoy together.
3. Pack an extra-special sack lunch on the day your child has a difficult test at school.
4. Surprise family members by turning back their beds, fluffing up the pillows, and placing a mint on their pillows.
5. Make a young child feel special when a baby brother or sister comes home from the hospital. Since a new baby usually

HIS NORMAL—HER NORMAL

special events

Consider the conflicts between you and your spouse that stem from the different ways your families celebrated special occasions like Christmas and spent vacations when you were growing up. Discuss assumptions you both brought into your marriage about "normal" ways families celebrate special occasions and view vacations and holidays. Listen and learn from each other; then negotiate your way to the "new normal" for your relationship. (See examples below.)

His Normal	**Our New Normal**	**Her Normal**
I grew up in a family that loved to celebrate. We sent out dozens of Christmas cards each year to family and friends across the country. I think staying connected to family and friends is so important.	We will decide which occasions are most important to us and why they're important, and we will celebrate within our budget.	I grew up in a family that never had much extra money to spend on "frivolous" stuff. I didn't have many birthday parties and didn't go to many. I think we should save our money rather than spend it on unnecessary gifts and cards.
His Normal	**Our New Normal**	**Her Normal**

FROM THE HEART

Sometimes the best family traditions have nothing to do with holidays or special occasions but evolve from memories of your own child-hood. Remember snow days when you were a child— waking up to a world transformed overnight into a vast playground? Snow days for our children meant "Good-bye, routine!" The boys would leap around the room, call friends, pull their coats and boots out of the hall closet, and head for the great outdoors. Faster than I could say, "Keep those gloves on!" the Peels' briefly pristine yard was a maze of boot tracks, snow-fort walls, and snowmen. In the kitchen, Bill pulled out the heavy artillery: deep pots for chili that could hold ample servings for drop-ins.

receives a lot of attention and presents, buy your child a present and carve out some focused time to spend together.

6. Make a "Welcome Home" banner for a family member who has been out of town. Place it in front of your house to celebrate his or her arrival.

7. Draw a warm bath for a family member who has had a hard day. Warm and fluff a towel in the dryer.

What Will Your Children Remember?

Envisioning is important. Your children are not going to grow up remembering if your floors were always spotless and the family room perfectly decorated. They *are* going to remember vacations, special occasions, and out-of-the-ordinary events— and if Mom and Dad were fun, positive people to be around.

Imagine it's the future. Your children have grown up and left home. What do you want them to remember about family occasions and vacations? Use the space below to record what you would like them to say about you.

When I was growing up, vacations, holidays, and celebrations usually meant my mom . . .

_____

_____

_____

_____

When I was growing up, vacations, holidays, and celebrations usually meant my dad . . .

_____

_____

_____

_____

When it came to traditions and celebrating holidays and occasions, our family . . .

_____

_____

_____

_____

8. Offer a toast to honor a family member's accomplishment. "To Mary Beth, whose hard work paid off. Congratulations for winning the spelling bee today!"

9. Have a first-things celebration. Make a big deal out of a child's first bicycle ride without training wheels, first tooth lost, or first day at a job.

10. Turn an ordinary weekend into a minivacation at home. Choose a weekend and block it out on the family calendar. Stock up on groceries and snacks. Get out board games, and rent a few family movies. Turn off all phones and put a sign on your front door that says your children can play after your minivacation. Keep chores and cooking to a minimum. Plan some fun Saturday outings everyone will enjoy.

SMART MOVE

Make a pact with your spouse to be alert for the little things your family can celebrate.

QUICK FIX

QUESTION: *Whenever we go on vacation, my husband takes along his laptop and BlackBerry. He checks in with his office at every pit stop and several times a day at our destination. Meanwhile, the kids spend much of their time, both in the car and even at the hotel, bent over their portable game systems. How can we tame technology when we're on the road?*

ANSWER: Call a family meeting before you leave. Discuss, negotiate, and come up with agreed-upon expectations for how much "screen time" will be allowed and how many times e-mail will be checked while you're on vacation. Turn it into a game by establishing fines for noncompliance. Dad has to pay a fine to the kids if he exceeds limits, and they have to pay a fine to you if they go over their limit. Earning spending money from Dad's fees and not losing anything they receive by paying fees of their own is a big incentive to keep the rules. Bring along a small timer they can use to help monitor themselves and their dad.

11. Decorate your dining room with streamers and balloons for a spur-of-the-moment celebration.
12. Eat by candlelight to make a dinner extra special one night.

cost-saving vacations

Odd, isn't it, how vacations can bring out the worst in everyone? You and your spouse are stressed from working up to the last minute on things that need to be done before you leave. As you back out of the driveway, the kids are bouncing all over the car in anticipation of that first horseback ride or hike up the mountain. You're not even on the highway before they ask for the first of many times, "How much longer till we get there?"

As Bill mentioned, we endured more than a few stressful vacations before learning some lessons that continue to make our family vacations a lot more fun. Family getaways have the power to refresh and renew—physically, relationally, and spiritually. That's the good news. The even better news is that you need not overspend to make it happen.

But a fun and refreshing vacation doesn't happen by accident—and it obviously won't happen at all unless you believe, even in a shaky economy with little money for extras, that getting away as a family for rest, relaxation, and recreation is vitally important to the health and well-being of your family and its members. Numerous medical and psychological studies have reported the benefits of time away and the hazards of not taking it. Even the Bible stresses the importance of rest. It would have been easy for people living on a subsistence level in an agrarian society to place a low priority on allocating time for rest and relationships. But God made it clear that He is serious about regular rest breaks from the work routine. The Gospels record at least six times during Christ's short ministry when He retreated across the Sea of Galilee or into the wilderness for time away from His work.

Taking a week or two off in the summer for a lengthy time away with your family may not be a cure-all for an ailing family atmosphere, but it can be a good start at building relationships, making positive memories, and inaugurating new rituals for relaxation and refreshment. And if you're scratching your head as to

CAUTION!

If you don't disconnect from the world, it's hard to connect with your family in meaningful ways. Impose a moratorium on electronic devices, except for certain designated times during your vacation.

GOOD TO KNOW

The U.S. National Park Service oversees about 400 sites, including 58 national parks and 75 national monuments.

Road Trip Planner

Make your next family car trip a team effort. Brainstorm with your spouse how you can make travel time an enjoyable experience for all.

Estimated Travel Time _____

Entertainment Ideas	Travel Schedule
BOOKS	SIGHTSEEING
GAMES	
AUDIOBOOKS/CDS	
DVDS	
TRAVEL BOX & SUPPLIES	
PICNIC FOOD & SNACKS	

FROM THE HEART

Adventure always
involves risk. What
if you risk going
on a family rafting
trip and it rains the
whole time? Well,
now you know you
won't repeat that—
without checking
the weather forecast
first. But you might
discover, as we did,
that recalling such a
trip—how miserable
we were and how
stupid we looked,
drenched and
standing on the side
of the road holding
a raft over our heads
while trying to hitch-
hike back to our
car—makes us laugh.
Ironically, disasters
like this can go a long
way to forge family
bonds.

how you're going to pay for it, start a vacation fund and turn it
into a family project. Brainstorm as a family about simple ways
to save here and there to meet your goal. Put a big jar in a central
location. Start a routine of collecting loose change each day to
add to the jar. One study reported that Americans carry $1.28 in
change. If you saved that much each day for a year, you'd end up
with $467.20. Organize a family garage sale; encourage kids to
sell unwanted toys and gear on eBay or Craigslist. Small amounts
add up over time.

Just because your family can't fly to the Caribbean this year
doesn't mean you can't have a great vacation. And an added
benefit is that you can turn all the research, planning, and saving
into some great teachable moments for your kids—about practical details and decisions (age appropriately, of course), but
more important about creativity, contentment, and commitment
to your priorities.

Drawing from the victories and defeats, successes and failures
of over 30 years of family vacations, I share five Peel family vacation rules.

1. Like any project, a vacation doesn't materialize on its own.
   Don't wait until the last minute to prepare. Talk through
   details together and create a plan. Set your departure date
   and work back. Discuss how and who will research and who
   will follow through with actions—make reservations, print
   boarding passes, service the car and fill it up with gas, gather
   children's gear, and such. Shared work on a common goal is a
   good part of the joy.

2. Scour the Internet for coupons and travel discounts. There
   are lots of family travel deals out there (at least one upside of
   the down economy). Research which local restaurants at your
   destination have coupons and kids' menus.

3. Pack your sense of humor and a positive attitude. This will
   help you survive bad weather, rude people, poor service, and
   a host of other inconveniences.

4. Give yourself permission to relax. A vacation won't change
   your life in a week, but it can be refreshing if you let it be.
   Don't fall prey to free-floating guilt that says you should
   be working or doing something more useful, or that you
   shouldn't be having such a good time.

5. Do less than you think you can during the trip so that no one comes home exhausted. Schedule alone time for family members who need it.

Whatever your family's special event, remember: calamity and confusion happen. Food burns, sinks back up, tires go flat, flights get canceled, and the power sometimes goes out. Rise to the circumstances. In addition to the memories being made, you're passing along something even more important than a flawless event: the life skills your children absorb when you adroitly field whatever comes along.

So how can you determine what memorable family traditions, special events, and vacations to pursue? The ACT worksheets that begin on page 159 can help you decide. The time and energy you invest in activities and events that encourage togetherness, mutual enjoyment, and positive memories will reap big rewards.

THE MOST IMPORTANT THINGS TO REMEMBER

1. Like any project, hosting a birthday party or holiday celebration requires planning, research and development, delegation, follow-through, and deadlines.

2. Don't wait until you have enough money to plan the perfect party. If something is worth celebrating, it's worth celebrating no matter how simple the event.

3. Every child's mind is a museum of memories.

4. Traditions and common experiences cement a family. There's something about being able to say, "This is the way our family always does it."

5. Share the work, as well as the joy. The idea is to promote family bonding and team spirit—and to make memories that last.

6. Don't expect your children to be perfect just before or during your special event. Hang on to your emotions and deal with misbehavior calmly and in private.

7. People are more important than any occasion. Dropping everything to console a sad child is a lot more important than making sure your table decorations are perfect.

8. Sometimes it's better to carry on a tradition that's been scaled down rather than go to either of two extremes—dropping the occasion completely or doing it so big that your stress meter reaches the danger zone.

9. Accept the fact that calamity and confusion are often uninvited guests at celebrations. Food will burn, toilets will overflow, and your power may go out. But you can still make positive memories if you are able to laugh about mishaps and plans that go awry.

10. You don't have to wait for a new year, a new month, or better circumstances. There is no better time than now to start creating positive memories for your family.

11. Spending time and/or money to build relationships and create shared memories is a good investment.

special events department

Take a few minutes to think about the key causes of stress in the Special Events department of your home. You and your spouse should use a different color pen or pencil to circle the number that best describes your individual stress level for each topic.

Key: 1=No Stress; 5=Very Stressful (0=Not Applicable)

Party/event planning	0	1	2	3	4	5
Kids' birthday party planning	0	1	2	3	4	5
Holidays	0	1	2	3	4	5
Christmas	0	1	2	3	4	5
Family celebrations	0	1	2	3	4	5
Photo organization	0	1	2	3	4	5
Gift giving	0	1	2	3	4	5
Greeting cards	0	1	2	3	4	5
Vacation planning	0	1	2	3	4	5
Travel with kids	0	1	2	3	4	5
Family fun time	0	1	2	3	4	5
Date nights/getaways	0	1	2	3	4	5
Other _____	0	1	2	3	4	5
Other _____	0	1	2	3	4	5
Other _____	0	1	2	3	4	5
Other _____	0	1	2	3	4	5
Other _____	0	1	2	3	4	5
Other _____	0	1	2	3	4	5
Other _____	0	1	2	3	4	5
Other _____	0	1	2	3	4	5
Other _____	0	1	2	3	4	5

special events department

Your Priorities

Look again at the items in the previous chart that you ranked as a 4 or a 5. Then you and your spouse should read the "I want" statements below and place a check in the box next to the ones that best describe your priorities for managing the Special Events department in your home. Circle two or three that you each deem most important.

I want ...

his	hers	
❑	❑	to celebrate and capture special moments of our family life.
❑	❑	to create and carry on family traditions for important holidays.
❑	❑	to put making positive memories high on our priority list when spending our time and resources.
❑	❑	to not be so overwhelmed with trying to make an occasion special that no one has any fun.
❑	❑	to keep decorations on hand for spur-of-the-moment celebrations.
❑	❑	to always have greeting cards, gifts, and wrapping supplies on hand.
❑	❑	to display and archive our photos so we can enjoy them now and for years to come.
❑	❑	to have fun and creative birthday parties our children will always remember.
❑	❑	to have an annual garage sale.
❑	❑	to take at least one great family vacation every year.
❑	❑	to go on weekend outings as a family as much as possible.
❑	❑	_____
❑	❑	_____
❑	❑	_____

Your Goal

Consider your individual and shared priorities, then write an overall goal that reflects your desires for the Special Events department. For this purpose, think of a goal as a broad, general, timeless statement that describes your overall aim for this department. Sometimes it is helpful to begin by identifying the key words that you'd use to describe this department when it runs well. Here's an example:

> **Key Words:** *positive memories, happy occasions, family traditions*
>
> **Goal:** *To plan occasions and events to celebrate the special moments of life and carry on family traditions; to watch for opportunities to make positive family memories.*

Key Words: _____

_____

Goal: _____

_____

special events department

Using this worksheet, divide up responsibilities for the Special Events department.

Who's Responsible for What?

Responsibilities	Who does it now?	Who else could do it?
Plan/coordinate birthday celebrations	_____	_____
Plan/coordinate Thanksgiving	_____	_____
Plan/coordinate December holiday events	_____	_____
Plan/coordinate other annual holidays	_____	_____
Plan/coordinate other celebrations—weddings, showers, graduations, reunions, religious occasions, etc.	_____	_____
Decorate for holidays and special occasions	_____	_____
Plan and prepare for family vacations	_____	_____
Plan memory-making family outings	_____	_____
Organize neighborhood activities	_____	_____
Plan and oversee garage sales	_____	_____
Buy gifts	_____	_____
Keep gift-wrapping center stocked	_____	_____
Send greeting cards	_____	_____
Plan weekend outings	_____	_____
Other _____	_____	_____
Other _____	_____	_____
Other _____	_____	_____
Other _____	_____	_____
Other _____	_____	_____
Other _____	_____	_____
Other _____	_____	_____
Other _____	_____	_____
Other _____	_____	_____
Other _____	_____	_____
Other _____	_____	_____

eight: managing yourself

A lot in our culture has changed—for better and for worse—since I began writing about family management 21 years ago. At least three things have changed about a Family Manager's job. For one, husbands are doing more housework. A study from the University of Michigan shows that men perform about 13 hours of housework per week now, compared with six hours in 1976. You've probably noticed the changes yourself. Maybe your husband washes dishes most nights or folds laundry on Saturdays—something your dad rarely did when you were growing up. (By the way, women now perform about 17 hours of housework, compared to 26 hours in 1976.)

Second, homeschooling is more accepted in mainstream circles. An estimated one to two million children are homeschooled in the United States. And for every homeschooled child there is a parent—usually Mom—who has taken full responsibility for her offspring's education, another obligation on top of her already packed Family Manager job.

A third change is that more moms are choosing to leave the workforce and stay home with their kids. Where such a choice might have been ridiculed two decades ago, women have become more tolerant and even supportive of fellow moms staying home instead of staying on a career track. The most recent U.S. census figures show 5.3 million families with stay-at-home moms, up from 4.5 million families in 1994. The so-called mommy wars seem to have settled into a comfortable truce.

Whether a woman works exclusively from home or heads to an office each day, self-management often slips to the bottom of her to-do list—and not only because of limited time. When a mom

GOOD TO KNOW

According to the results from six major studies on happiness, women's overall level of happiness has dropped, both relative to where they were forty years ago and relative to men.

Say Good-Bye to Mommy Guilt

Although full-time motherhood has become more valued recently as a culture-affecting vocation, many women who have chosen this path still struggle at parties or gatherings when they're asked the dreaded, inevitable, identity-validating question: What do you do? Since much of our culture, especially in large cities, is focused on work and the marketplace, many women find their transition to stay-at-home mom more difficult than they expected. Deep down they know that the types of caregiving tasks—changing diapers, wiping noses, playing Go Fish—that now fill their days are vitally important.

But when former colleagues ask questions like, "What do you do all day?" feelings of doubt can creep in. Moms start asking themselves, *What am I doing with my education?* or *Am I losing myself—my old career self—in the identity of motherhood?* Somehow organizing a playgroup or leading a den of Cub Scouts doesn't seem to matter as much as organizing a board meeting or leading a marketing presentation.

If you're wondering why you bothered to earn a graduate degree when you're surrounded by young people instead of professionals, try to reframe your thinking. You're not wasting your education, training, and experience—you're building on it. And you're passing along your life experiences to your children. Try to think about the seasons of motherhood. That's admittedly easier for me now that I'm on the empty-nester side, but you can do it. You won't always be changing diapers and wiping up spit-up squash—you'll be celebrating an independent child who moves and eats and thinks on her own. You won't always be potty training toddlers or washing sheets after another overnight accident—one day you'll move from one activity to the next without asking, "Do you need to go potty?" When you complete one stage of motherhood, you move on to another with its own challenges and rich rewards.

While stay-at-home moms have traditionally battled guilt over "wasting" their education, many moms who are employed outside the home have had to contend with their own guilt. They may constantly feel pulled—when they're home, their minds keep going back to all the work piled up in their offices; when they're at work, they may long to be with their child—perhaps rocking an infant to sleep or picking up a child after school. Sometimes these working moms also feel judgment from relatives and neighbors who hint at all the sacrifices their families are making so Mom can stay at home.

Perhaps the one lesson we've all learned is that it is usually impossible—and pointless—to judge another woman's motives for staying at home or joining the workforce. Personally, I am thankful that women have so many options—staying home, working outside the home, working from home, or even starting a business from home. Every family needs to choose what's best for them—not based on what everyone else is doing or expectations from friends and grandparents or pressure from the workplace.

starts to feel less valued at home than she did in the office, she may start to underestimate her worth. Once she's less certain of herself, she may stop taking care of herself—and rationalize her inaction. The mom employed outside the home may find it easier to soothe her stress with a candy bar than a jog around the block after dinner. Whatever your day job—whether you're paid in sticky kisses or company stock—self-neglect leads to a dangerous downward spiral.

I can't pinpoint the exact time I realized that, for each of us, managing life—our responsibilities, relationships, and resources—is all about managing ourselves. We need to know who we are becoming—the kind of women we want to become and what we need to become the women we envision. We also need to determine if we are making the best use of our resources, whether our time, money, energy, or God-given talent. Once again, this boils down to knowing what we value most in life—our first things—because what we value defines us.

Whether you're 22, 62, or someplace in between; male or female; empty nester or riding herd on a passel of kids, you have two things in common with every other person on the planet: you will be older next week than you are this week, and you will not be the same next week as you are this week.

So, who are you and who are you becoming? Do you see your-self as a valuable person, worthy of care? How do you care for your body? How are you developing your skills and sharpening your mind? Are you growing in your faith?

self-care is not gender specific

For years, when I've written and talked about self-care, I have focused almost exclusively on women—because a woman typically fills the role of Family Manager. But self-care isn't gender specific. Women and men both need to practice deliberate self-care to keep their minds sharp, bodies agile, and spirits nourished, which in turn makes them better spouses, parents, friends, and professionals.

Self-care doesn't have to be solo either. Most mornings, Bill and I pray and walk together. This is a special time reserved just for us, and we both benefit. We stretch our bodies, strengthen our faith, and reconnect with one another. We're taking care of ourselves and each other.

GOOD TO KNOW

According to a 2009 poll conducted by AOL and *Woman's Day*, 57 percent of women say they would prefer to quit work and stay home with their children.

CAUTION!

Failing to make self-care a priority can damage your health. Excessive stress produces cortisol, which can cause weight gain, heart problems, and even dementia-like symptoms, according to recent studies by the Center for Brain Health at the University of Texas at Dallas. Cortisol buildup can create memory loss and a lower attention span, and it is particularly toxic to the memory area of the brain.

GOOD TO KNOW

More than 60 percent
of American adults
do not exercise
regularly.

SMART MOVE

Walking 2,000 extra
steps a day will
help keep pounds
off. Walking 6,000
additional steps a
day (about three
miles) is the point
at which pounds
really start coming
off, according to
researchers at
the University of
Colorado.

We also recognize that my idea of self-care doesn't always coincide with Bill's—and vice versa. So we allow each other time to recharge our batteries in different ways. I find refreshment in things like rearranging the furniture or accessories in a room, which translates into unrefreshing work for Bill. I also enjoy sitting outside with a good book and taking classes on topics that stimulate my thinking. Bill gets recharged by building things with his woodworking tools, working with our sons on creative projects, and going on fly-fishing trips with other guys. We make a concerted effort to allow each other times such as these.

I have a friend who's a busy mom and wife with a demanding professional career. Every Sunday afternoon she heads to the café in her favorite bookstore. She can actually feel her shoulders relax as she walks through the door and smells the aroma of coffee and new books. After a few hours of reading and journaling, she leaves reenergized for another week. She might have abandoned this simple pleasure years ago except that her husband encourages her to go. He makes sure that time is built into the family's Sunday schedule. In turn, she gives her husband a pass on housework or yard work during Penn State football games. After cheering on his favorite team, he is ready to tackle the next item on the family's to-do list.

Another frugally minded friend cuts corners everywhere she can so she can allow herself a day out twice a month when a housecleaning service comes. She says it's worth every penny to walk back into a clean house.

How well do you and your spouse know what kinds of activities replenish each of you? It's important to know this about each other, to encourage each other (without nagging) to take time for self-care, and to make sure your family schedule allows for refreshing activities you can do together and individually. Doing so will make you better marriage partners and better parents.

adding energy to your life

Self-care does not need to be expensive or time consuming. If you haven't made it a priority, build one of the following ideas into your schedule as a way to add energy and joy to your life. Even small routines and rituals can make a significant difference in the quality of your life and relationships.

- Create a morning ritual. Begin each day by building in time to read a portion of the Bible or a devotional book. If you have a long commute, consider listening to a Bible or devotional on CD during your drive. Thank God for the gift of the new day. Ask Him to help you live wisely and experience His presence in everything you do.
- Practice relaxation techniques. Consciously relax your brow. Drop your lower jaw. Avoid clenching your fists or holding tightly to objects; consciously relax your hands.
- Give yourself a facial at the end of a long day.
- Exchange foot massages with your spouse at the end of a long day.
- Listen to music that calms your spirit when tackling onerous chores.
- Create the routine of getting together on a regular basis with a few friends who encourage you. For example, maybe eat lunch together on the first Tuesday of every month.
- Set aside time to brainstorm how you might use your skills and education to launch a part-time business from your home.
- Listen to soothing music or inspirational audiobooks in your car. Or learn a foreign language via audio curriculum.
- Give yourself and your spouse permission to get massages when you're beat.
- Find a mind-sharpening game or activity that you and your spouse can enjoy together. Bill and I play word games like Scrabble and Boggle frequently.
- Take a class and learn together. A few years ago Bill and I enrolled in a yearlong course on worldview and ethics. We enjoyed reading the same books and working on the same assignments.
- Don't overschedule your weekends. Plan for free time to do something you enjoy. Block it out on your calendar just as you would an important appointment, and honor this commitment to yourself.
- Create a restful atmosphere in your bedroom. Train yourself to view it as a place to rest and relax. Don't do office work in there. Make your bed as comfortable as possible. If your pillow is uncomfortable, replace it.
- If you can't take a vacation someplace right now, take a vacation from something. A half-day vacation from e-mail

SMART MOVE

Studies show that a massage may boost your immune system.

GOOD TO KNOW

In 2008 the average U.S. health club charged $35 a month for membership.

and phone calls is rejuvenating. A vacation from television and radio can help clear your mind. If the atmosphere at home or at the office has become negative, set the pace for positive change by deciding to take a vacation from complaining or making negative comments for 24 hours.

Life does not stand still. We are constantly changing. The choices we make every hour of every day will determine whether we are older and *better* next week than we are this week—and next month, next year, and next decade. Sometimes it's hard to remember this when you have a preschooler pulling at your shirttail, older children involved in multiple activities, and a husband who's not sure what to do with his life. We all must keep reminding ourselves that we have immeasurably more to offer to those who need us when we take time to care for and develop ourselves.

habit breakers–habit makers

In 2003 Bill ran a marathon and I ran a half marathon. Running is on my short list of least favorite ways to exercise, and I have the thighs to prove it. I signed up and trained with Bill because he had always wanted to check off "run a marathon" from his list of accomplishments. I knew it would be all too easy for him to shut off the alarm, roll over, and dream about the 6:00 a.m. Saturday morning training sessions instead of actually attending them, so in the spirit of team togetherness, I trained as well.

I was placed in the "Overcomers" group (i.e., slow and inexperienced), but there were lots of us, so I wasn't too humiliated. By the third week we were jogging three miles at a slow pace, but every step was difficult. As the trainers pushed us each week to go a little farther, they promised we would get to the point where it felt good. Amazingly, they were right. But it took a while to get there. And more amazingly, I finished 13.1 miles.

Our experience reminded me of the value of spouses working together to achieve a goal or establish a new and healthier habit for their family. When you change your behavior and undertake a new action for 21 consecutive days, you will begin to form a habit. I've found that on the 22nd day, it is harder not to do the new habit than it was to make the change on the first day.

After reading this book, you or your spouse may have realized you've fallen into some habits you would like to change. Use the seven departments to help you think through different areas of your home and life. If you would like to make some changes, jot them below. They don't have to be big things. Many times small changes make a big difference. Choose one to start working on together, and do it for 21 days. On the 22nd day you'll have a new habit.

Time and Scheduling:

Home and Property:

Menus and Meals:

Family and Friends:

Finances:

Special Events:

Personal Management:

finding time for self-care

Carving out time for self-care and personal development is like that: it's often hard on the front end. But it gets easier. The key is to stay with it.

At least one thing is democratic in every time zone for every person around the globe: a day is a 24-hour affair. And in America, at least, a woman decides for herself, consciously or unconsciously, to run her 24 hours or to be run by them.

Mind you, "run or be run" is never a single choice. We're talking myriad small choices—each and every day—that request our time and attention, until finally, further down the road, our good judgment becomes more reflexive. Even then it's easy to be blindsided, interrupted, and then surprised one morning when we wake up and realize that we've defaulted back to pushing self-care to the bottom of our daily to-do list.

Speaking of staying with it, will you hit pause right now and fetch your new best friend (your legal pad, notebook, journal, day planner, or computer screen)? If this talk of limited time and taking

GOOD TO KNOW

The best time to nap is between 2 and 3 p.m., which should boost your energy without interfering with your ability to sleep well at night.

QUESTION: *When I don't sleep well, I start off the day in a bad mood and things get worse the rest of the day.*

ANSWER: Talk yourself into a positive start to the day. If you get up complaining about feeling sluggish or dreading the day ahead, those thoughts will inform your day and cast a negative tint on everything. But if you decide that it's going to be a great day, despite your lack of sleep and the ill-tempered client you're meeting with later, it's easier to stay on top of circumstances and enjoy the day. This may sound silly, but you'll find that it really works.

control of yours has piqued your interest even a little, now's the time to brainstorm your first things.

Don't edit yourself; just write. If you could do or be anything at all, what would it be? What is it you hate doing? What complaints do your children and/or spouse have about the family? Be brutally honest; refuse to kid yourself or write to please your inner judge or anyone else. No one is looking. Don't cheat yourself.

Now review your brainstorming and hone your list of what matters to you and your family. Do your first things turn on certain talents and gifts? on caring for your body? on growing in your faith? on returning to school? on spending more time with like-minded girlfriends? on traveling and learning? on sports? on writing a book? Please know this: when you love and care for yourself (not narcissistically, but appropriately and healthily), you are better able to love and care for others. So when you're ready, remind your spouse of this truth and read your list aloud. Ask him to think with you—and modify your list only if you agree with his observations. (Be honest!)

When you're ready, tape your work inside a cupboard door, and for the next 40 days, as a demand, request, surprise, or opportunity arises, match it against the list. There's no right or wrong here. These aren't more rules: you're forming a habit of choosing to keep first things first.

Determine Who You Will Become

Every day we are presented with many choices. How we choose to spend our minutes—the mini-choices we make—determines how we change our lives.

We make small decisions such as:

Will I choose to turn on the TV or ask my spouse to go for a walk?

Will I nag my spouse about something that is irritating me or choose to focus on his or her strengths?

Will I work at my computer or play a game with my kids?

Each decision can make a big difference in the long run. The old adage is true: first we make our decisions, then our decisions make us.

Use this worksheet to list small choices that could make a big difference in your family.

Choices I *usually* make

_____
_____
_____

_____
_____
_____

_____
_____
_____

_____
_____
_____

_____
_____
_____

_____
_____
_____

Choices I *should* make

_____
_____
_____

_____
_____
_____

_____
_____
_____

_____
_____
_____

_____
_____
_____

_____
_____
_____

SMART MOVE

Don't add unnecessary stress to your life. Whenever possible, plan major life changes—moving, remodeling, marrying, having a baby, your mother moving in, your spouse changing jobs—so they do not occur at the same time.

10 Simple Ways to Refresh Yourself

1. Join a book club or Bible study group.
2. Linger over lunch with a friend.
3. Plant a small garden.
4. Escape on a romantic weekend with your husband.
5. Volunteer for a cause you're passionate about.
6. Register for a continuing education course.
7. Enroll in a ballet class.
8. Swim at the Y three times a week.
9. Finish the needlepoint pillow you started five years ago.
10. Read a book for pure enjoyment.

a man's point of view

managing yourself

According to the latest statistics, nearly three-fourths of mothers with school-age children work outside the home. Whether your wife is holding down two jobs—one outside the home and her Family Manager job—or is occupied with the business of running your home as the full-time Family Manager, it's likely that she's tired a lot of the time. Mothers live a life of perpetual motion, rising early to get the family up, clean, dressed, fed, and off to where they need to be. Then after a day of work, moms have to squeeze in grocery shopping, picking up the children, cooking dinner, cleaning up the kitchen, doing additional housework—and then there's the kids' bedtime routine. Small wonder if there's less and less romance at the end of the day.

By now I hope you've reviewed the "Who's Responsible for What?" lists in chapters 2 through 7 with the 140 or so jobs that have to be performed for an average household to run well. If you have, pat yourself on the back because you now understand what it takes to manage a home and family. I also hope that you've started to step up to the plate and swing away at some of the responsibilities, lightening your wife's family management load.

While the first six Family Manager departments have a way of clamoring for attention, the seventh—personal management of the Family Manager herself—is without a doubt the most neglected. In other words, the physical, intellectual, emotional, and spiritual care and development of your wife often get crowded out, and that's not good.

It's in the very nature of motherhood for women to put everyone else's needs above their own—until they burn out, that is. And when that happens, family life will come tumbling down—on your head. Having let Kathy get to the place of extreme burnout, I can tell you from experience, you don't want to go there. Not only was I suddenly overwhelmed with all the pieces I needed to pick up, I felt no small amount of guilt for letting things get so bad in the first place. The truth is, people need time to recharge their batteries. As a husband, you need to make sure to monitor your wife's stress level and help her take regular care of herself. You need to do whatever it takes to guarantee that your wife has time for herself—doing things that rejuvenate and enrich her life.

You may object: you work hard all day and need a break when you get home. I would suggest that so does she. If you don't understand why a former loan officer who became a stay-at-home mom to care for her 10-month-old is dishrag limp at the end of the day, here's an assignment: send your wife away for a weekend with girlfriends while you take care of the house and your 10-month-old. It will be an enlightening (and exhausting) experience, but you'll be a better husband and father for doing it. And don't just do it once. If you let her neglect caring for herself over time, the price you will pay for her burnout will be far higher than what it would have cost you to take preemptive action. Here's an old adage you and your wife need to take to heart:

If your output exceeds your intake, then your upkeep will be your downfall.

SMART MOVE

Create your own spa experience at home. You can download recipes for homemade body scrubs, facial masks, and body creams. Turn down the lights in the bathroom, light a candle or two, put on relaxing music, and of course, do this when the kids are someplace else.

 HIGHLY RECOMMENDED

In addition to encouraging your wife to escape occasion-ally, you also need to take time to monitor your Family Manager's stress level on a regular basis. Create an occa-sion when you can have some quiet, uninterrupted time together. Ask her to identify the biggest current stressors in her life. If this isn't the first time you've done this and if you are not one of her biggest stressors at the moment, you can also share your stressors with her. The His Normal–Her Normal worksheet (see page 175) may also reveal some sources of friction between you.

Next, ask her to visualize the kind of woman she would like to see in the mirror a year from now. Make a list of her comments. How would she like to change for the better? If she doesn't mention anything, ask her to think about all the following areas: physical, emotional, social, and spiritual. Then ask her what you and your family can do to help her reach her objectives. Write down her ideas. If she hasn't done so yet, ask her to complete the worksheets at the end of this chapter. If you think she would prefer to complete this exercise together, volun-teer to work through the process with her. Help her come up with a plan. Then consider how you can assist her in reaching her goals. This will involve not only helping her find time but supporting her in the new things she wants to include in the found time you are helping her create.

signs of burnout

Charity and self-management begin at home. Your family will cele-brate the day when you master *your* clock and calendar. She who is puffy eyed, snappish, habitually harried, falling into and out of bed, in the fast lane to burnout, forever forming excuses about why she doesn't take care of herself, yet grousing about how she looks and feels sets the standard by which the rest of her family lives.

Sorry, but it's true.

HIS NORMAL—HER NORMAL

self-management

Think about the conflicts between you and your spouse that stem from the different ways your parents modeled taking care of themselves physically, mentally, socially, and spiritually. Discuss assumptions that you both brought into your marriage about the "normal" ways people take care of themselves. Listen and learn from each other; then negotiate your way to the "new normal" for your relationship. (See examples below.)

His Normal	Our New Normal	Her Normal
My family wasn't nearly as physically fit as my wife's, but we were readers. My dad is in his mid-70s and is sharp as a tack. I think that's so much more important than being in top shape physically. And besides, I hate to work out.	We want to stay sharp both physically and mentally, so we'll schedule activities that are good for us physically, as well as activities that will improve our minds.	I grew up in a family that admittedly was over the top about physical fitness. My mom and dad still look great in their 60s, and I want the same to be true of me when I'm their age.
His Normal	**Our New Normal**	**Her Normal**

CAUTION!

Depression is the second most debilitating disease for women (heart disease is first), according to the World Health Organization.

GOOD TO KNOW

Medical studies suggest that the ideal amount of time for adults to sleep is seven to eight hours a night.

Take it from one who learned the hard way how critical it is to deflect second- and third-thing requests. As I mentioned in chapter 2, an up-and-down nod to the wrong thing is a no to the best thing. And it's one more tired step on the road to losing everything.

Run with me through this list of burnout symptoms:

- fatigue
- insomnia
- mental lapses
- headaches
- irritability
- rashes
- loss of sexual interest
- ulcers
- regular illness

Between self-mastery and burnout is your ability to keep first things first, to put time you've blocked out for nurturing yourself in the *stat* column. And here's the irony that bears repeating: when you say no

- someone else gets a chance at the work;
- people respect you more as they see you stay increasingly within your boundaries;
- you feel better and have more energy because you're taking care of your body;
- your life is fuller because you're stretching your mind; and
- you become more loving, joyful, peaceful, patient, kind, gentle, and self-controlled because you are bearing the fruit of Christ's Spirit through spending time with Him.

The first no is scary. People who are used to a yes from you won't like a no. We all have a pushy person or two in our lives. You know the type: when she learns that you turned down her request to work at the school carnival because you're going on an overnight silent retreat, she tells you, after she has told others, that you made a selfish decision. She'll get over it, and so will you. What's more . . . although you don't like your reflection in the asker's eyes, turn and see yourself in your family's eyes. Enough said.

The key to self-management is self-mastery. And self-mastery

QUICK FIX

QUESTION: *My sister often shares some great Bible verse or quote from her morning quiet time with me. I always smile and nod, but inside I feel so guilty. I've tried starting a quiet-time routine several times but just never seem to stick with it.*

ANSWER: Nowhere in His Word does God command people to have a "daily quiet time." However, He does tell us that His Word should be on our hearts and minds continually. In fact, I think drawing on the wisdom, power, and compassion of our Creator is one of the most basic forms of self-care.

One woman may value setting aside a half hour or so each morning to bring her schedule, praises, and requests to God before having to deal with anything or anyone else that day.

Another woman, though, considers herself a quiet-time failure because she never gets past Leviticus when trying to read through the Bible. She may bring a devotional to the kitchen table at breakfast, only to realize as she scrapes up her last spoonful of milk and cereal that she spent the whole meal skimming the newspaper.

Do you know the major difference between these two types of women? The first woman views her quiet time as an opportunity to connect deeply with her beloved Friend; the other likely sees it as a to-do item that she needs to check off her schedule to keep God happy.

If you identify with the second woman, you don't need to feel guilty or stuck. Instead, why not consider how God created you and then ask for His help in finding ways to remain aware of His presence and in His Word? Maybe your heart really soars when you're singing or listening to a Scripture passage set to music. Perhaps you find yourself interacting with God most deeply as you wrestle with your deepest fears or a difficult Scripture verse in your journal. Or you may find yourself marveling at God's creative genius as you stand watering the eye-popping blooms in your front yard.

Keep searching for ways you can communicate with God continually, particularly through Scripture. But never assume that God will bless and use you only if you've had your quiet time that day. I like what Jerry Bridges says in his book *The Discipline of Grace*: "Your worst days are never so bad that you are beyond the *reach* of God's grace. And your best days are never so good that you are beyond the *need* of God's grace."

SMART MOVE

If you don't already do so, start journaling. Putting things down on paper—whether it's ideas, goals, prayers, or things you don't want to forget—will help solidify your thoughts and remind you of what you want to do, who you want to become, and what you want for your family.

GOOD TO KNOW

The top six self-care splurges for moms, according to a survey from www.babycenter.com, are:

1. Time to yourself to recharge your batteries
2. Clothes that make you feel gorgeous
3. Sweet treats—especially if you don't have to share
4. Beauty boosters—massages, facials, manicures, and pedicures
5. Quality time with your spouse
6. A brief escape from reality, such as reading a magazine not about parenting or going to a movie by yourself

starts with self-understanding. Before you can manage to find time on the clock for yourself, you must know what makes you tick. Ask yourself:

1. What gives me energy?
2. What drains my energy?
3. What do I find myself putting off that I really want to do?
4. What time of day am I at my best?
5. What motivates me? (On a list of tasks, what do I want to do first?)
6. What frustrates me or causes me to lose my temper?
7. When I feel happiest, what am I doing?
8. When I solve a problem and enjoy doing it, what skills am I using?
9. What do other people compliment me on?
10. What skills do other people say I have?
11. When I lose track of time enjoying a task, what am I doing?
12. If I could do anything at all, what would it be?

Ever consider mapping your days by your preferences and energy levels? Does it seem indulgent? It's *smart*. On planet Kathy, for example, energy cometh in the morning. (I long beat myself up for feeling lethargic at night.) So why not—oh, I don't know—*play to my strengths*? Knowing what I know now, if a special national vote were held and I were suddenly elected president, I'd sign no treaties or bills after 10 p.m. My cabinet would know to schedule all high-level meetings before noon. In serving myself, I'd better serve my country.

As it is, back in Dallas as a mere voter, I know to kick in my to-do list well before breakfast, and I just say no, mostly, to hard thinking after 7 p.m.

And something else about me: I'm more simultaneous than serial. That is to say, I prefer to check off a couple of things at once. Yes, this subjects me to family ribbing. But in my enlightened state, I know that a single day never exceeds 24 hours, so I stay alert for opportunities to combine chores.

For example, I read the news and magazine articles while I'm on the elliptical machine at the gym. I read a chapter in a novel (I am rereading all of George MacDonald's works this year), carefully turning pages while I'm getting my nails done. I often wear ankle weights while puttering around the house. Of the many advantages to double-tasking, the greatest is the time gained for moments that *do* get my full attention: writing in my prayer journal, hearing my son James recount his day at work, helping Joel or John create marketing strategies for their businesses, calling a friend who is going through a difficult passage and praying with her over the phone, or preparing for an intimate rendezvous with Bill.

You may not like your tasks in twofers. A good friend of mine, who is more focused, thorough, and meticulous than I, insists on doing one thing at a time. Another friend ridicules my early hours in only the nicest way. She's a night person and does housework from eleven at night until one in the morning. Still another friend invented one of the first daily planners just for women. Her days come in 15-minute increments, which she plans with military precision. When, over lunch, we compare notes and ideas, we're amazed at how differently two people approach the same 24 hours and yet maintain a high level of productivity.

Let's reconsider the first time-management truth: there is no perfect system; and the second time-management truth: any system beats no system. To fit in time for your own care and personal development is to live by first things. (The worksheets beginning on page 181 can help you determine what those priorities are.) To live by first things is to break the boilerplate approach and exchange it for an increasing knowledge of one's unique and ever-growing self. That's the call: to most fully and authentically and confidently live no one's life but your own and to become the woman God created you to be. This is not a call to selfish preoccupation. In order to be all you can be for the people God calls you to serve, you have to take time for your own self-development.

The call to manage yourself well, you see, is a high calling.

FROM THE HEART

Between the demands of family, friends, work, and more, finding time for yourself may often seem impossible. In reality you do have the time; it's up to you, however, to intentionally allocate some of it to taking care of yourself.

THE MOST IMPORTANT THINGS TO REMEMBER

1. At some point you must realize that if things are going to change, then you have to change.

2. Self-care is not a call to selfish preoccupation but a necessity to be all you can be for the people God calls you to serve.

3. You have to be in good shape to give good shape to the rest of your life.

4. When your own needs go unmet, your body gets stressed and starts reacting. Your mind races in turmoil, your emotions are erratic, and your spirit becomes discouraged. You are in no condition to nurture anyone else.

5. The next time you're tempted to put your own needs on the back burner, try to remember that your children do not need a cranky, tired, resentful mother.

6. Making fitness a priority isn't just about looking great. It's about caring for your one and only body in a way that promotes and increases health, energy, and longevity.

7. You make decisions, and then your decisions make you.

8. When you work in harmony with the way God created you—instead of trying to be like someone else—you can better manage your home and personal life.

9. No matter how out of control you feel, your life can change in significant, positive ways.

10. Little changes can make a big difference.

11. If you aim at nothing, you'll likely hit it.

self-management department

Take a few minutes to think about the key causes of stress in the Self-Management department. You and your spouse should use a different color pen or pencil to circle the number that best describes your individual stress level for each topic.[1]

Key: 1=No Stress; 5=Very Stressful (0=Not Applicable)

	0	1	2	3	4	5
Personal appearance	0	1	2	3	4	5
Fitness/exercise	0	1	2	3	4	5
Eating habits	0	1	2	3	4	5
Weight loss	0	1	2	3	4	5
Spiritual development	0	1	2	3	4	5
Continuing education	0	1	2	3	4	5
Hobbies/recreation	0	1	2	3	4	5
Health/wellness	0	1	2	3	4	5
Lack of sleep	0	1	2	3	4	5
Self-care habits	0	1	2	3	4	5
Stress management	0	1	2	3	4	5
Friends and social connections	0	1	2	3	4	5
Work/rest balance	0	1	2	3	4	5
Life focus/purpose	0	1	2	3	4	5
Work outside the home (paid and/or volunteer)	0	1	2	3	4	5
Self-esteem	0	1	2	3	4	5
Other _____	0	1	2	3	4	5
Other _____	0	1	2	3	4	5
Other _____	0	1	2	3	4	5
Other _____	0	1	2	3	4	5
Other _____	0	1	2	3	4	5
Other _____	0	1	2	3	4	5
Other _____	0	1	2	3	4	5
Other _____	0	1	2	3	4	5

---

[1] This is the one department where you cannot delegate! You must take responsibility for taking care of yourself. For that reason, no Tackle Tasks as a Team is provided. However, it is important to encourage one another and give each other permission to do what's personally most replenishing.

self-management department

Your Priorities

Note the topics you ranked with a 4 or a 5. Now read the "I want" statements below and place a check in the box next to the ones that best describe your priorities for managing yourself. Circle two or three that you each deem most important.

I want . . .

his   hers

his	hers	
❑	❑	to develop to my full potential.
❑	❑	to take good care of my body and remind myself regularly of my inestimable value.
❑	❑	to follow my physician's suggestions regarding checkups and tests.
❑	❑	to be a lifelong learner.
❑	❑	to nurture and develop my strengths.
❑	❑	to carve out time every day to do something that refreshes me.
❑	❑	to attend college or get more professional training.
❑	❑	to start my own business.
❑	❑	to learn a new skill.
❑	❑	to exercise regularly and eat wisely.
❑	❑	to schedule times for personal recreation and fun with friends.
❑	❑	to meet new people and make new friends.
❑	❑	to nourish my soul daily and grow in my faith.
❑	❑	to be purposeful about how I live my life.
❑	❑	to spend time daily in prayer and meditation.
❑	❑	_____
❑	❑	_____
❑	❑	_____

Your Goals

Since this chapter deals with self-management, you and your spouse should first consider your individual priorities and then each write a statement that reflects your personal goal for the Self-Management department. For this purpose, think of a goal as a broad, general, timeless statement that describes your overall aim for this department. Sometimes it is helpful to begin by identifying the key words that you'd use to describe this department when it runs well. Next, list common personal goals you share and how you might work together to accomplish them. Record at least one shared goal. Here's an example:

> **Key Words:** *healthy body, learning, spiritual development, recharge my batteries*
> **Goal:** *To do something every day that is good for my body; to learn something new every day; to grow in my faith every day; to schedule times regularly for personal recreation and refreshment.*
>
> **Shared Key Words:** *healthy bodies, grow in faith*
> **Shared Goal:** *Join a couples hiking club; tag-team babysit so we can each attend a women's or men's Bible study.*

Key Words: _____

_____

Goal: _____

_____

Shared Key Words: _____

_____

Shared Goal: _____

_____

nine: family team-building workshop

I hope that after reading this book you and your spouse understand the value of partnering together like never before. I hope you are beginning to divvy up household tasks and negotiate your way to expectations you both can live with. Maybe you are encouraged that you've started communicating in healthier ways, and you're invigorated by the plans you've already made and the goals you've set for positive change.

Now, however, you may be wondering how to get buy-in from your kids about the concept of family teamwork. Perhaps you expect your 12-year-old to protest when you ask her to set aside a few hours Saturday afternoon so you can teach her how to do her own laundry. Your eight-year-old may not understand why you will no longer make an extra trip to the grocery store just because you've run out of his favorite juice boxes. And if your family is anticipating a major event, such as a cross-country move, your children may be more apprehensive than excited about all the upcoming changes and upheaval.

If you think that your kids may need some coaching and encouragement about operating as a family team, or if your family is contemplating any kind of a big change or project—from making fairly drastic changes in everyday housecleaning routines to uprooting and moving to a new city—consider setting aside some time to plan and hold a management workshop on an upcoming weekend. It might be one of the best things you ever do.

Organizations use workshops for a number of reasons, such as teaching people new skills, planning intensively for new projects, giving people who will be working closely together a chance to

CAUTION!

I've never met a Family Manager who didn't meet with at least some resistance to getting her family to work more like a team. I sure did. I found that identifying the resistance is the easy part. It's looking for ways to overcome the resistance that takes time, energy, and tenacity—not to mention duct tape over my mouth.

get to know each other's strengths and weaknesses, and forming a coherent team. A workshop can achieve similar purposes for your own family. Consider the following benefits of conducting a workshop for your home team:

A Dozen Team Benefits

1. Two (or more) people can accomplish more than one. It's simple arithmetic—two people times two hours of cleaning equals a clean house, an attic or basement where you can actually find things, or a formerly trashed SUV that's neat as a pin on the inside and waxed to a high gloss on the outside.
2. An overwhelming task often becomes manageable when it's shared. That's true for tangibles that one person can't do alone, like moving furniture around, as well as intangibles like brainstorming ways to trim the budget.
3. When you work together, you finish sooner and have more time to spend as a couple or a family doing things you enjoy.
4. Working as a team helps to develop important skills—cooperation, communication, sensitivity—in children (and their parents), preparing them to be better team members at school and work.
5. No one person has all the skills and abilities needed to manage a family. A team allows family members to focus on individual strengths and do fewer things they are not good at.
6. The family team provides a safe and loving environment in which to learn new skills and abilities.
7. A team approach stimulates commitment to the family. Someone who is not required to help usually doesn't value the family.
8. Working together is usually more fun and always more encouraging—we're in this together!
9. Teamwork provides daily opportunities for family members to demonstrate trust and confidence in each other, to show appreciation, and to build up that invaluable asset—self-esteem.
10. More than one head working to solve problems from different perspectives makes for more creative solutions.
11. Since no one person is trying to do everything, all of you will have more energy to overcome obstacles.
12. The family that works together is there for each other. A great blessing of a family team is having people to go through the good times and the bad times with you.

As a family, look for other ways to live out the truth that "two are better than one." Not only will you share the load, but you'll multiply the pleasures along the way.

- *You give your kids a chance to discuss both their frustrations and the things they think are working well at your home.* Everyone gets to have input—thus, buy-in—to new ways of doing things. This prevents kids' frustration at having something thrust on them that they didn't have any say in and didn't agree to do. This also creates less stress for the Family Manager because she doesn't have to feel pressured to think up all the answers or be an "enforcer."

- *Your children will feel like valued members of your family team.* It's a well-known fact that happy employees are those who feel empowered by bosses who listen to their concerns and allow them to figure out how to do their jobs—rather than being told exactly when, where, and how they are to perform. These employees feel as if they have control over their lives and "own" part of the results of their work. Kids are no different. They will appreciate that the workshop is not just about what Mom and Dad want to change but an opportunity for them to express their desires for change too.

- *You can "market" the cause of family teamwork and share your vision of working together to make your home a good place for all*—not a magazine-cover specimen, but an orderly, sanitary home where everyone contributes and the burden does not fall heavily on any one person. You can also emphasize benefits and explain how a team is a group of people who work together for the common good of all of them. For example, you could bring up a time in the past when you worked together to bring about positive change. "Remember that time we all worked together to get the house ready for Joel's birthday party? We all felt proud that the house looked so good—and we were able to find things for a change. Wouldn't it be great to have it looking like that on a regular basis? We could have parties more often!"

- *You have the time to explain how to do certain tasks—which can go a long way to reduce frustration later.* Instructions like "Just do your best" or "Help around the house more" are too general. Spell out the tasks for kids in as much detail as possible; for example, "Place all recycling in the blue bin and regular trash in the gray bin on Friday morning before school, and roll the bins to the curb. Return the bins to the garage when you get home from school." You can also encourage

GOOD TO KNOW

In The *Effective Executive*, leadership expert Peter F. Drucker observes that there will always be more productive tasks for tomorrow than there will be time to do them. He urges business leaders to determine which tasks deserve priority rather than allowing the pressures to make the decisions. To do this, he offers these guidelines:

- Pick the future over the past.
- Focus on opportunities, not problems.
- Choose your own direction rather than jumping on the bandwagon.
- Aim high for something that will make a difference rather than something that is safe and easy to do.

Consider what following these principles might look like in your family.

SMART MOVE

A business manager does not expect employees to get a job done without the necessary tools of the trade. Make sure your kids are equipped to do the chores for which they are responsible. If you want them to keep their clothes off the floor, put a small laundry basket in their closet for dirty clothes and lower the closet rod so they can reach it. You might also want to install child-level pegs or hooks for hanging jackets, pajamas, and other often-worn items.

QUICK FIX

QUESTION: *Our two sons, 12 and 14, spend most of their time in school or with their traveling sports teams. Since they don't have a lot of free time, my husband and I aren't sure how much we should expect them to help around the house. How would you go about making that decision?*

ANSWER: Certainly you want to be sensitive to the fact that your kids need time to decompress after the stress and structure of their daily schedules. But after a short nap or 30 minutes of TV and completed home-work, if they still have time for TV or computer games or other recreation, then they have time to help around the house. No matter how busy their schedules, everyday tasks like picking up their bedrooms and belongings, as well as cleaning up after themselves in the kitchen and bathroom, should be givens. Assigning jobs like taking out the trash, putting away their laundry, and helping with dinner cleanup isn't asking a lot of them either. As for chores that require more time, you might require that they do one or two over the weekend.

family members to be creative in developing their own ways to accomplish jobs. Be sure to show your support and model a positive attitude. When someone has a new idea, your first response should be "Try it and see if it works," not "That will never work!" (Within reason, of course: a creative way for a child to clean her bedroom is not shoveling everything under the bed.) You may have a visually motivated child who likes to be able to see where things are kept. If she shows a proclivity to organizing things in the basement where things are on open shelves, you might consider installing open shelves in her room.

- *You can talk about creative ways to mesh family members' skills and hobbies and chores.* For example, a teenager who likes to drive the family car may realize she could drive more if she ran errands for Mom or Dad. A younger child who likes to work in the kitchen might be put in charge of making the orange juice from concentrate for weekend breakfasts.

- *You'll have more brainpower available to solve problems.* Of course, there are private issues that should be discussed behind closed doors, but there are many problems—how to cut back on spending, how to make mornings less stressful, how to adapt to a family member's illness—that you can brainstorm about together. When a challenging situation is approached with an attitude of "what can *we* do to solve it," not only will this allow the best possible solution to be implemented—because everyone affected by the problem is involved in finding answers—but it will also promote a spirit of unity.

- *You can work out win-win scenarios for potentially volatile situations.* If you suggest a decluttering campaign and a child expresses angst because he doesn't want to put away a model sailboat he's been building a little at a time or destroy next month's science fair project that's coming along nicely, you can discuss possible scenarios where everyone wins. Perhaps you decide that he can keep his model going on a card table in the corner of his bedroom, and you agree to clear a place in the garage for working on his science fair project.

- *You can learn the incentives that your kids value most—* whether it's an extra half hour of computer time or permission to hold a sleepover—for completing their responsibilities at home. Or if you're holding a workshop because a tight budget has forced you to cancel your cleaning service, what "compensation" can you offer your new cleaning service (aka your family)? Lunch out and a few rounds of miniature golf or bowling on Saturday afternoon after cleaning the house in the morning?

- *Everyone can brainstorm about how to make jobs fun.* You might decide to divide into teams, set the kitchen timer, and have contests to see whose team, Mom's or Dad's, can clean the kitchen faster for a week. Keep a tally of scores and offer a night or two off regular kitchen duty as a prize. Or have a clutter contest: give each family member a trash bag, set the timer, and at the end of 15 minutes, see whose bag weighs the most. Offer a prize to the winner.

GOOD TO KNOW

According to Sandra Hofferth, director of the University of Maryland's Population Research Center, in 1981, children ages 9 through 12 reported spending 5 hours and 18 minutes a week on such activities as repairs, meal preparation and cleanup, pet care, and outdoor work. By 2002, that figure had shrunk to 3 hours and 5 minutes.

- *You have a great opportunity to boost morale, show support, and express confidence in your family's ability to do a good job.* Positive expectations create an atmosphere for better performance.

pulling off your workshop

Decide what you'd like to cover at your workshop, how much time you should set aside for it, and where to hold it. You can hold a workshop at home, but you also might pick a weekend when you can get away someplace with a retreat atmosphere. You might rent a cabin or camp out at a state park that offers lots of fun activities. You might even follow the workshop with another family activity (such as a night at a water park). Finally, after finding an opening in your schedule, get the workshop date on your calendar.

Once you've worked out the logistics, detail what you hope to cover at your seminar. But a word of warning: if you've identified every change that needs to be made and you're ready to write an exhaustive procedure guidebook that covers every possible chore, routine, and stress-relieving operation for 365 days a year, my advice is: settle down. You want to build a team, not start World War III. The more you try to change at once, the less likely you are to succeed. Remember, even the houses on *Extreme Makeover: Home Edition* aren't built in a day.

topics for change

You might bring up one or two particularly regular and frustrating situations during your first workshop. For example, when our two older boys were 8 and 12, every time we got ready to go someplace they argued over whose turn it was to sit in the front seat. Their almost daily duel was wearing mightily on my nerves, so we brainstormed and came up with a plan where each boy would have a turn sitting in the front seat for one month. They knew on the first day of each month it was the other brother's turn, and they kept track of this themselves. Of course, when they got their driver's licenses, it was no longer an issue.

When picking topics for your workshop, try thinking of it like this: traffic control engineers identify certain city intersections where accidents occur and then put up traffic lights or warning signs to reduce the risk of collision. With that in mind, look for

Rewards for Responsibility

Your family will need to decide how to reward children for work done around the house. In our home, we did not give our sons monetary rewards for everyday chores. But when, as teens, they did a job that went above and beyond the normal call of duty (e.g., putting insulation in the attic to cut down our utility bill, painting a room, scrubbing mildew off the ceiling of a porch), we paid them.

When they were younger, I rewarded extra chores with chits, gold stars, and such, which could eventually be traded in for things like lunch out with Dad or Mom or a special outing. We also scheduled "fun" errands after a day of hard work, so that washing and vacuuming the cars without complaining might be followed by a trip to get a bike tune-up and new tires.

Not all rewards need to be tangible. Don't discount the value kids get from knowing they accomplished an important job or from receiving your thanks and recognition. And be sure to periodically reward the entire family team when you finish a big job together.

SMART MOVE

Just as leaders create buy-in by having employees partici-pate in decision making, you can help your kids—even younger children—be more enthused about cleaning by letting them equip themselves for the job. It's amazing how much more likely a seven-year-old girl is to remember to wipe out the tub after her bath (and avoid leaving a bathtub ring) if you let her pick out bubble bath and her own special sponge at the store. (As the water drains out she can use the sponge to swab the sides of the tub.)

problematic intersections in your home; for example, where chores that need to be done frequently collide with stress or bickering. Brainstorm routines you can put in place to act like traffic lights and warning signs.

For instance, you might start off by saying, "I want the laundry room to be clean, and I want the kitchen to be cleaned once a day." Then your 12-year-old says, "I'd like to be able to invite friends over after school, but since Dad works at home now, I wish there was one room where we could hang out and not get in trouble if we get a little noisy. I'd also like to know that when I'm hungry the odds are pretty decent that I can find something good to eat." Dad chimes in with, "I'd like to walk into the family room and not find crusty bowls that once held ice cream." And your five-year-old blurts out, "I wish we could play Chutes and Ladders every night after dinner!" Practice active listening during the workshop. Truly focus on what each person is saying.

If your home is running fairly smoothly, you might think about something that is working well and how you might make it work even better. Say you have the routine of grilling hamburgers every Saturday night. You've been doing it so long you don't ever think

FROM THE HEART

As soon as children are able to help around the house, they need regular chores. Even a two-year-old can fold towels and pick up toys. Toddlers won't fold the towels as neatly as you'd like, but that's okay. It's more important that they learn to be productive. Children need to see themselves as active contributors to the welfare of the home since they benefit from living there.

about what you're going to have for dinner on Saturday nights. It's a ritual your family enjoys. Why not instigate some other no-brainer menus, like pasta every Tuesday?

Sometimes routines that have been working for a long time and still seem to be working can use some fine-tuning as family circumstances change. Suppose you've always cleaned the house by working together on Saturday mornings. You all work pretty well together and generally everything is done by noon. Basically this is not a "broken" system. But if someone on your team suggests that you could get just as much done if you all cleaned a half hour every evening, which would leave Saturday mornings free, you might well discuss changing your cleaning routine.

Businesses generally work on fixing the most critical problems first. If morning chaos is causing your kids to get tardy slips regularly, you'll want to start there. Or if finances are a big challenge, start there. Solicit ideas from everyone who's old enough to talk and think about how to spend less money. A seven-year-old may volunteer to have an at-home, less-expensive birthday party. A teenager may volunteer to buy her prom dress at a secondhand shop. Perhaps your energy bill has skyrocketed. One child might volunteer to be the family energy monitor and collect fines from family members who leave doors open and leave the lights on when leaving the house.

Be careful to broach topics without being critical or overly negative. You might begin by stating a problem, saying something like, "I've been thinking we haven't been sitting down to eat dinner together as a family very much anymore. I'd like to know how you feel about that." If they respond with blank looks or by saying that things are fine with them, tell them, kindly, why it's not fine with you—that you're concerned about falling out of touch with each other and about not eating healthy food at a decent hour. You might also tell them why this is a problem now when it wasn't before—for example, you've been working longer hours and you haven't had as much time to fix dinner lately. Or it might be that you really don't like to cook that much and are fresh out of ideas for good, nutritious meals and simply want some help with the cooking and shopping.

Once your family agrees on solutions to address your biggest annoyances, you can use the Launching Routines worksheet (see page 191) to track them. For instance, perhaps at the workshop you mention your frustration at always trying to decide at the last

Launching Routines
(Standard Operating Procedures)

Hundreds of tasks are required to keep a family going. Launching routines can make everyone's life easier. Once you decide how, when, and by whom something should be done, you eliminate a lot of questions and arguing. Spend time as a couple thinking about recurring problems or stressors in your home, then think about how you might create a routine to alleviate each problem.

Recurring Issue/Problem   **Routines**

Time and Scheduling

_____   _____
_____   _____
_____   _____

Home and Property

_____   _____
_____   _____
_____   _____

Menus and Meals

_____   _____
_____   _____
_____   _____

Family and Friends

_____   _____
_____   _____
_____   _____

Finances

_____   _____
_____   _____
_____   _____

Special Events

_____   _____
_____   _____
_____   _____

Self-Management

_____   _____
_____   _____
_____   _____

minute who will drive your sixth grader to and from play practice—
an exciting, but unexpected, addition to your family's schedule
since she landed the leading role. You may decide to create a
driving routine: you or your husband will drive her on weekdays,
and your teen will drive her on weekends. Or perhaps clutter is a
problem, so you agree to establish the routine of setting aside the
first Saturday in each month for family decluttering. You can create
routines for just about anything, and they can save a lot of time
and angst.

workshop logistics

A couple of weeks before the workshop, let your family know
what you want to accomplish. Let them know you'll want their
input to show that everyone's opinion counts. Create anticipation
by promising surprises, appetizing snack breaks, free time, and
prizes as rewards for participation.

A few days before the workshop, be sure you have all the
supplies you'll need:

- a flip chart or giant sticky-note paper and markers for
  brainstorming
- a notebook computer or legal pad for the recording secretary
- the proper clothing
- games
- prizes
- food and beverages

In the spirit of teamwork, you might give each family member
a list of things he or she will be responsible for gathering by the
morning the workshop starts.

Wherever you gather, make sure all electronic devices are turned
off. Begin by playing an old favorite or new game and then talk
about the way you play together, which is a great team-building
exercise in itself. Who's most competitive? Who likes to play with a
partner or on a team? Who enjoys going it alone?

Select someone to act as the recording secretary and take notes
whenever you are discussing ideas. When you have a specific topic,
like deciding how the laundry gets done or when the house gets
cleaned on a regular basis, brainstorm and let him or her jot down

your ideas. Using giant sticky-note paper is ideal because you can post what was recorded on the wall afterward.

Solicit everybody's opinions about the need for change. Then ask for suggestions about what would work. At this stage, all ideas, no matter how far out, are fodder for the discussion. Don't dismiss any ideas as silly. Simply list them all. Then you can group them into categories and discuss the relative merits of everything from eating out every night (probably not a reasonable option) to sharing cooking chores on a regular rotating basis—maybe week by week or night by night. If it's week by week, the person who's cooking the following week could, with your help if necessary, plan menus the week before. The shopper, whether it's you or someone else, would then have a weekly list. In this scenario, after his or her week in the kitchen, the cook would move to the cleanup crew.

Depending on the size of your family, you may also want to schedule small-group working sessions. Perhaps you and your husband decide to take some time to work on an allowance and rewards structure while your children create a new chores schedule, reflecting the decisions you've made. Or you might want to delegate to them the task of coming up with a system of rotation and sharing that gets the kitchen and the bathrooms cleaned regularly. Make sure you plan time for frequent breaks, especially if you have younger children.

Whatever plans you make, be as realistic and as simple as possible. Don't make overly elaborate arrangements you know you're not capable of following. Be sure that children are assigned, or volunteer for, age-appropriate parts of the system.

swot for success

If there's a specific goal you want to achieve, change you want to make, or big project you need to orchestrate, it's important to identify the resources that will help you achieve your goal, create a smooth transition amid change, or complete a big project successfully. It's also important to be aware of roadblocks that could get in the way. A SWOT analysis can help you do this. This tool was developed by Albert Humphrey, a business researcher and consultant based at Stanford University.

SMART MOVE

At your workshop, ask each family member this question: "In your opinion, what would make our home a good place to be?" Be willing to listen to everyone's comments, and don't roll your eyes or react harshly if they are outlandish. "You know we can't afford a swimming pool. That's a ridiculous idea!" is actually a ridiculous way to respond. Better would be, "Boy, I would like to have a pool someday too." Even better would be, "I've also been thinking lately that swimming would be fun. There are some good weekend deals on at hotels right now. Let's see if we can scrape together enough money to spend a relaxing weekend at one soon."

SWOT stands for Strengths, Weaknesses, Opportunities, Threats. It is used to identify and evaluate the internal and external factors that are favorable and unfavorable to a project's success. The box below shows the kinds of ideas and information to record in each box of a SWOT analysis.

For example, let's say your husband receives the promotion he has been working hard for, but his new job will require a transfer to another city. Your first step is putting your home on the market. You agree that you want to sell your home for as much as possible, so you set an objective to get your home ready to put on the market by a certain date. A SWOT analysis at your workshop will help you see the strengths and assets that will help you achieve your objective, and the obstacles or limitations you'll need to work around.

Here's an example of a SWOT analysis you might create for the moving scenario above.

Objective: To get our home ready to put on the market by April 30 in order to sell it for as much as possible	
Internal	
Strengths (assets and advantages)	**Weaknesses** (limitations or disadvantages)
➤ Home is generally in good repair ➤ Great location, good schools ➤ Three kids old enough to help paint ➤ It's spring so we can plant annuals and enhance curb appeal	➤ Faucet needs to be replaced in kids' bathroom; no one feels competent to do it ➤ Backyard landscaping needs work ➤ April is really busy for all of us; time to work on the house is limited
External	
Opportunities (resources and possibilities)	**Threats** (obstacles from outside forces)
➤ Spring/summer is a good time to sell a house—lots of people moving ➤ A great Realtor who knows our neighborhood ➤ Good neighbors ➤ A friend who is a home stager can help us get ready for the first open house ➤ A friend who's a handyman might help with small repairs	➤ Three other houses on our street are on the market ➤ Housing market is soft ➤ Home loans are harder to get ➤ Timing: we have to sell our home before we can buy one in the new city

workshop follow-through

Pick a day to start your new routines. Mark the occasion with some kind of celebration, even if it's only a small ritual of hanging the schedule on the refrigerator door or offering a toast to the new chef for a delicious dinner. For the first few weeks after your workshop, set up a regular weekly time, perhaps after dinner on a weeknight or on a Sunday afternoon, to solicit feedback on how the changes and new routines are working. Use this time to make adjustments as necessary and to reemphasize that you're a team doing some new things together or doing the familiar things in a different way. Make it clear that honest mistakes are allowable; new methods take time to adapt to until they become second nature.

Keep in mind, every change affects all parts of an organism, which in this case is your family. As you institute change in one area, make sure you're not causing a problem somewhere else. If a new routine is for your 12-year-old to vacuum the house before he leaves for school on Thursdays, make sure this is not a morning when your husband sleeps in because he worked the night shift. That one seems obvious. But sometimes it's the obvious that escapes our notice. As you start new routines, be aware that you'll likely want to fine-tune them as you go. Maybe in a flush of enthusiasm your eighth grader volunteered for more chores than she can actually do. (Well, it has been known to happen.) Or maybe a new routine is working just fine until your teenager starts Advanced Placement English and has three hours of homework every night. Periodic review and adjustment of routines is good for everyone.

Use the tips below to foster continued family team spirit:

- *Update chore lists periodically.* Make sure each family team member has an opportunity to raise the issue of switching jobs as his or her skill level and schedule change.
- *Remember that challenging assignments are good.* Be sure to cheer your team members on in their pursuits.
- *Expect imperfect work, but shower praise for effort.* "You did an excellent job of washing the dishes. Now just try to remember to clean out the sink after you've finished."
- *Reward the completion of certain tasks in age-appropriate ways.* Depending on the recipient, a special dessert, a later bedtime that night, or an evening with the car may be appropriate.

SMART MOVE

A family member with an artistic bent can create a way to keep your family's goals and priorities front and center. Post (or perhaps even frame) them in a visible place to provide everyone with a quick reminder of what's most important.

QUICK FIX

QUESTION: *I'm so tired of my husband and kids promising to help me clean the house the following Saturday, only to disappear early that morning with a friend or stay glued to the television, promising over and over that they'll help "just as soon as this show is over." What can I do?*

ANSWER: It's easy to recognize that your family is spending more time in front of computer and TV screens than working together as a team. Doing something about it—besides nagging everyone to turn off the computer or TV, threatening to cut the power cords, or playing the martyr's role ("I'm the only one who cares about our family")—is the challenge.

While it's easier to vent your anger by scouring out the bathtub—and grumble while you try to handle every other chore on your own—that kind of response doesn't satisfy anyone or encourage team building. Neither does going ballistic or trying to guilt your family into cooperating. Patience, a positive attitude, and creative ideas for family fun are your secret weapons. That's why I recommend working as a team to clarify each family member's desires, expectations, and responsibilities. A family workshop is a great way to do it. *The Busy Mom's Guide to a Happy, Organized Home* also contains helpful tools, such as a breakdown of age-appropriate chores for children and a parent/teen contract.

Finally, make sure you're building in time for enjoyable family activities. Knowing that you'll all be taking a bike ride to the local ice cream shop once the house is clean can be a powerful motivator.

- *Cover for each other during busy times.* Your children will appreciate your doing some of their tasks during busy times such as exam week. They can return the favor and do some extra chores when you have a big deadline at work.
- *On a regular basis, make time for fun, team-building excursions.* You may decide to set aside regular times for

family workshops. Three times a year—at the beginning of the school year, at the New Year, and at the beginning of summer—are three natural times to review your household procedures.

Holding a workshop is a great way to initiate the idea of teamwork to your whole family. The Family Workshop Retreat Planning Guide on pages 198–204 is designed to help lead you through the process.

Keep in mind, though, that change takes ongoing work. Some days you will likely feel as though working as a team is more work than doing things by yourself. On those days, I urge you to remind yourself that good family management and good family teams are about developing the best in all of you, not just about washing dishes and folding clothes. Knowing how to operate as a member of a team is a valuable skill—and building strong, loving relationships and a happy, organized home is, well, invaluable.

There will be days—maybe even weeks—when you feel like you're not getting anywhere. When expectations aren't met, talk about why, and how you got off track. If the discussion gets heated, remind yourselves of your Couple's Communication Covenant (see page 14)—a good thing to share with your kids.

But on many, even most, days, you'll reap the rewards of your family workshop, as you work more like a team in a cleaner, cozier, calmer home. You won't be feeling frazzled because you're trying to do it all yourself. You won't be feeling martyred. You can, and should, pat yourself and your team members on the back for making your family a place where everybody works together.

SMART MOVE

Start the routine of meeting once a week—for just 10 minutes—to review how things are going and to make adjustments to assignments and schedules. You will likely find that your family likes talking about their roles in making your home a better place for all of you.

family workshop planning guide

If you are planning a family workshop, these notes will lead you through the process. Of course, feel free to adapt them to better fit your needs. You can download additional copies of these guided notes at www.familymanager.com.

before the retreat

Sit down with your spouse and begin discussing those pressure points or recurring frustrations in your home that are causing stress among family members. Choose one or two (no more than three) to focus on at the retreat. Use the questions below to help you as you plan.

In what ways would you like your family to operate more as a team after this workshop?

_____

_____

_____

What problematic areas/household routines would you like to address?

_____

_____

_____

What is working well in your household? How can you express this to your family at the workshop?

_____

_____

_____

How could you add some fun to this family time?

_____

_____

_____

FROM THE HEART

As you prepare for the retreat, think about what is already working well in your home and family. Be prepared to share some of these positive points, along with one or two things you appreciate most about each person there. Doing so will start off your time together on a positive note.

logistical details

Date(s): _____

_____

Place and Contact Information: _____

_____

_____

_____

Supplies Needed: _____

_____

_____

_____

☆
SMART MOVE

When announcing the retreat to your family, be optimistic that it will be successful as well as fun, which is fundamental to enthusiasm, energy, and creativity.

at the retreat

Explain to your family what you hope to accomplish today. Let them know you'll begin by brainstorming together, which should then lead into specifics on new routines for your home. The following questions are meant to stimulate discussion as you brainstorm. Be sure to be clear that you value the input of every family member.

What is working well? _____

_____

_____

_____

What causes the most frustration? (Examples: laundry never gets put away, late to church, wet towels on bathroom floor)

_____

_____

_____

What would you like to see happen differently? What would be the positive and negative implications of such changes?

1. _____

    +: _____

    −: _____

2. _____

    +: _____

    −: _____

3. _____

    +: _____

    −: _____

4. _____

    +: _____

    −: _____

4. _____

    +: _____

    −: _____

5. _____

    +: _____

    −: _____

Begin brainstorming some ways you might rework some existing routines so they lead to the changes you want. Ask your family: Which routines that are working well could we adapt to the subpar or difficult situations in our home? Can you think of anything new we should begin doing? Record everyone's ideas, then choose the ones you want to implement. Ask for volunteers or assign different family members with the responsibility of overseeing implementation. For example, if pet hair is taking over your home and you're tired of vacuuming the family room almost every day, a teen might be assigned the vacuuming. You might then agree to his suggestion that he be able to ask a younger sibling to brush the dog and cat each day so he will only have to vacuum twice a week. List the details for each new routine you plan to launch in the spaces below.

assignments

Task: _____

Person Responsible: _____

Steps to Complete: _____

_____

_____

Task: _____

Person Responsible: _____

Steps to Complete: _____

_____

_____

Task: _____

Person Responsible: _____

Steps to Complete: _____

_____

_____

assignments *(continued)*

Task: _____

Person Responsible: _____

Steps to Complete: _____

_____

_____

Task: _____

Person Responsible: _____

Steps to Complete: _____

_____

_____

Task: _____

Person Responsible: _____

Steps to Complete: _____

_____

_____

Task: _____

Person Responsible: _____

Steps to Complete: _____

_____

_____

Task: _____

Person Responsible: _____

Steps to Complete: _____

_____

_____

small-group working sessions (optional)

This is a time when your family could break into smaller groups to discuss particular issues. For instance, you and your spouse might want to work out an allowance system while your kids decide how they want to rotate certain chores.

major family goal (optional)

If your family is facing a major transition or has a major goal to complete within the next six to twenty-four months, consider using a SWOT analysis to map out the strengths, weaknesses, opportunities, and threats this event will bring. (See example on page 194.)

Objective:	
Internal	
Strengths (assets and advantages)	**Weaknesses** (limitations or disadvantages)
External	
Opportunities (resources and possibilities)	**Threats** (obstacles from outside forces)

retreat wrap-up

Be sure to end your retreat by celebrating the progress you've made today. Asking a few final wrap-up questions will help you determine what changes family members are most excited about:

What did you learn at the workshop that surprised you the most?

_____

_____

What do you think is the best idea to come out of this retreat?

_____

_____

Let's set a date two to four weeks from now when we can get back together briefly to discuss how well we're making the changes we've agreed on: _____ .

post-retreat feedback

Begin by praising family members for positive steps you have seen them take since the retreat. Let them know that their feedback at the retreat was very helpful and that you want to follow up to be sure the family is working together toward your goals.

What is working well? _____

_____

_____

What adjustments do we need to make to our new routines? _____

_____

_____

Discuss the best ways for family members to let others know when a routine is no longer working or when they have an idea for making it run even more smoothly. _____

_____

_____

web resources for couples

These sites were last accessed in June 2009. While each contains helpful information, inclusion does not imply endorsement by the author or publisher of all the content on the Web sites.

couples resources/help

http://www.familylife.com
FamilyLife provides a wealth of information on marriage and family life, including help for sensitive issues such as infidelity.

http://www.marriagetoday.org
MarriageToday, founded by Jimmy and Karen Evans, offers articles geared for couples in many situations, from those considering marriage to those contemplating divorce. It also offers a magazine that can be viewed online.

http://www.nationalmarriage.com/marriage_counseling.asp
The National Institute of Marriage has intensive marriage counseling programs for struggling couples.

couples retreats/conferences

http://www.drgaryandbarb.com/home/the_great_marriage_experience.php
Dr. Gary and Barb Rosberg provide The Great Marriage Experience conference as well as materials specifically for military marriages (available under the "Group Involvement" tab).

http://www.familylife.com
FamilyLife offers the popular Weekend to Remember marriage conferences across the nation. Visit this site for information and other helpful resources.

http://www.garychapman.org
Dr. Gary Chapman presents the Toward a Growing Marriage conference in various locations across the country. Check this Web site for a current schedule.

http://www.intensives.com
The Hideaway is nestled at the rim of the Palo Duro Canyon near Amarillo, Texas. It includes beautiful scenery, great meals, and intensive sessions with professional marriage counselors.

http://www.marriagebuilders.com
Marriage Builders, founded by Dr. Willard F. Harley Jr., author of the best seller *His Needs, Her Needs*, offers the Marriage Builders Online Program; the *His Needs, Her Needs* study course; telephone coaching; and many articles by Dr. Harley.

http://www.nationalmarriage.com/marriage_conference.asp
The National Institute of Marriage offers The DNA of Relationships for Couples, a marriage conference that helps couples on their journey to a great marriage.

education and the arts

http://www.earlychildhood.com
Early Childhood is a resource for teachers and parents of children up to eight years old. It includes activities, articles, and crafts, as well as online radio interviews with education professionals.

http://www.eduhound.com
Eduhound provides a database of Web sites for "everything for education K–12," as the site states. They have tracked down information for everything you could imagine.

http://www.factmonster.com
Fact Monster, as its name suggests, gives you facts in every education category you can think of. You'll find games and quizzes and can even search facts by year from 1900 to the present.

http://www.familyeducation.com
Family Education categorizes its information by the age of your children, then gives information about school, life, entertainment, and special needs for each category. They've added a special touch for moms, providing games to give you a needed break.

http://www.funbrain.com
Family Education Network: Fun Brain is filled with educational fun for all ages.

http://www.pluggedinonline.com
Plugged In Online is a family-friendly site that provides ratings and reviews of movies, DVDs, music, television, and video games. Each review details both the positive and negative elements, along with any content that families should be aware of before using the media.

http://www.musictechteacher.com
Music Tech Teacher was created by a music teacher to provide teachers and students with lessons and resources for learning music technology and basic keyboarding. Many helpful links to other music Web sites are provided also.

http://www.nps.gov
The National Park Service provides information on all national parks, as well as some fun activities for kids like the NPS's Junior Ranger program.

http://www.scholastic.com
Scholastic provides helpful articles on school, reading, and parenting, as well as assistance with homework, handwriting, and much more. It also includes some fun activities you can do with preschool and grade-school children.

http://www.smithsonianeducation.org/students
The Smithsonian Institution provides this colorful Web site where families can study topics like people, art, nature, and science.

family connections

http://www.cozi.com
Cozi is a free Web service that allows you to keep a family calendar and make chore and grocery lists, which you can send as text messages to family members. The site even offers an iPhone app and can sync with Outlook.

www.dictionary.com
Dictionary.com offers a word-of-the-day feature your family can turn into a fun learning routine. Find it at dictionary.reference.com/wordoftheday.

http://www.dinnerdialogue.com
Family Matters: Dinner Dialogue is an excellent resource to help generate healthy discussion at the dinner table.

www.eduplace.com
Education Place is a good resource for brain teasers—good fodder for family dinnertime conversation.

http://www.evite.com
Evite is the leading social event planning site on the Web. It provides tools to help you plan and execute your event.

http://www.geni.com
Geni is a free private and secure Web site where you and your family can build your family tree. Only the people in your family can see your tree and profile.

http://www.jooners.com
Jooners provides a free online event sign-up service. You can have volunteers sign up to work shifts at a church function, or have family members sign up to bring items to a potluck.

http://www.lotsahelpinghands.com
Lotsa Helping Hands helps you create a free, private, Web-based community to organize family, friends, neighbors, and colleagues— a family's "circles of community"—during times of need. You can easily coordinate activities and manage volunteers with this intuitive group calendar. It also allows you to communicate and share information using announcements, messages boards, and photos.

http://www.yadahome.com
YadaHome provides a suite of tools to help you get organized. Just a few things users can do are share photos, create lists, search coupons, and join discussion groups. You can even have grandparents join and share recipes in your online recipe book.

family health

http://www.drwalt.com
Dr. Walt Larimore provides in-depth health assessments for your children and teens as well as a free eight-week family fitness plan.

http://www.mypyramid.gov
My Pyramid is an interactive tool created by the U.S. Department of Agriculture and the U.S. Department of Health and Human Services. It is designed to provide personalized nutrition guidelines based on a person's age, gender, and level of physical activity. Along with an introduction to the updated food pyramid, introduced in 2005, it is loaded with nutritional tips and resources for kids.

http://medlineplus.gov
MedlinePlus brings together authoritative information from the National Institutes of Health and other health-related organizations on a variety of health topics, diseases, drugs, and supplements. Users can also access an illustrated medical encyclopedia, interactive patient tutorials, and the latest health news.

https://familyhistory.hhs.gov/fhh-web
The Surgeon General: My Family Health Portrait is a tool to help you create a family health history report that you can save on your computer to give you and your health-care adviser needed insight about potential health risks.

financial help

http://www.budgettracker.com
BudgetTracker, Inc. enables you to manage your money online. It offers free basic service and paid subscriptions.

http://www.chaseclearandsimple.com
Chase: Clear and Simple gives excellent free resources to help you manage your finances successfully, including a student guide with lessons for teens on credit cards and budgeting.

http://www.christianpf.com
Christian Personal Finance is a blog site by Bob Lotich providing articles on finance and links to helpful information. He has an impressive amount of good current content.

http://www.crown.org
Crown Financial Ministries exists to help you experience financial freedom based on biblical principles. You will also find the Crown Money Map tool and be able to chat with a Money Map coach.

http://www.daveramsey.com
Dave Ramsey, host of a nationally syndicated radio show on finances, is the author of *The Total Money Makeover* and *Financial Peace University*. His Web site offers information on these resources plus more great financial information and tools.

http://www.echristianfinance.com
EChristianFinance helps users through free worksheets, financial calculators, articles, and Bible verses on money.

http://www.generousgiving.org
Generous Giving is a privately funded nonprofit organization that encourages givers of all income levels to live a life of generosity. The Research Library is an impressive database of articles and interviews on generosity.

http://www.masteryourmoney.com
Master Your Money provides access to years of financial expertise
from Ron Blue, posting frequent video answers to questions from
users.

http://www.mint.com
Mint is a free, award-winning online money management tool.

http://www.payjr.com
PAYjr offers a free online chore and allowance tracking system. You
can print chore charts and use the site to track the work your children do. The site then calculates what you owe your child. (Note:
The site provides an option to purchase a reloadable Visa Buxx card
to pay allowance to your teens.)

http://www.usatoday.com/money/perfi/calculators/calculator.htm
USA Today has gathered several online calculators all in one place
for calculations like "How much house can I afford?" or "How long
will it take to pay off my credit card?"

parenting

http://www.bethany.org
Bethany Christian Services offers support and resources about
adoption, both for those who are seeking to adopt and those who
are pregnant.

http://www.biblicalparenting.org
National Center for Biblical Parenting offers parenting seminars, closed e-mail support groups, phone coaching, and e-mail
parenting tips. The *Family Time Activities* books are a unique and
fun resource.

http://www.christiananswers.net/parenting
Christian Answers gives sound advice from well-known writers for
questions like, "What age should I potty train my child?" or "How
do I motivate my child to do homework?"

http://www.christianitytoday.com/momsense
Christianity Today's MomSense provides parenting information and articles geared toward moms but useful to both parents.

http://www.christianparentsforum.com
Christian Parents Forum is an online community of Christian parents. Healthy discussions about everything from raising toddlers to overcoming addictions can be found here.

http://www.covenanteyes.com
Covenant Eyes is an accountability software that reports Internet use and e-mails for selected users. It also filters unwanted content.

http://www.crosswalk.com/parenting
Crosswalk gathers fresh content from authors like Charles Colson and ministries like Insight for Living. There is an assortment of great articles and discussion forums.

http://www.familycorner.com
Family Corner offer advice from experts on important childhood issues, from teething to talking to your preteen about difficult topics. There are also recipes, craft ideas, games, coupons, and e-cards.

http://www.familyiq.com
Family IQ provides interactive e-learning courses, articles, forums, tests, and other resources to teach parents how to improve their parenting skills. There is a membership fee for full use of the site, but many articles can be viewed for free.

http://www.familylife.com
FamilyLife provides a wealth of resources for couples, including the highly praised Weekend to Remember marriage conference and the HomeBuilders studies. The site offers a free newsletter with a large archive of helpful information.

http://www.familymatters.net
Family Matters has articles on marriage and parenting, along with resources based on their conference Raising Truly Great Kids.

http://www.focusonthefamily.com
Focus on the Family is an online community where you can create a profile to start discussions and get information on relationships, marriage, entertainment, movie reviews, social issues, and life challenges. You can also listen to radio broadcasts and podcasts by Dr. James Dobson and others.

http://www.homeword.com
HomeWord (formerly YouthBuilders) has multiple tools for parents, including parenting seminars, free newsletters, and daily devotionals.

http://www.joniandfriends.org
Joni and Friends, founded by Joni Eareckson Tada, offers physical, emotional, and spiritual support and services to families impacted by disability. The site provides information on Joni and Friends' five-day family retreats across the United States, where families affected by disability can find hope and get a break from the challenges of everyday life.

http://www.kaboose.com
Kaboose provides sections on parenting, finances, crafts, games, holidays, food, and health. You may also participate in online community message boards. There are relevant pop-up ads but you can choose to "skip ad," and much of the content is worth the small annoyance.

http://www.lifeway.com
LifeWay provides articles for families, complete with a section dedicated to homeschooling. You will also find information about their publications, *HomeLife* and *ParentLife* magazines.

http://www.mops.org
MOPS International has an extensive network to support mothers of preschool-age children, as well as resources for free and for purchase. Find out how to locate or start a MOPS group in your area, and also learn about their annual conference, which is packed with great resources and workshops.

special focus

http://www.kyria.com
Kyria.com is a resource of Leadership Journal and Christianity Today International. Its mission is to equip women to use their gifts, take responsibility for their spiritual formation and the discipleship of others, and fulfill the work God has called them to.

http://www.militaryministry.org
Military Ministry, a division of Campus Crusade for Christ, offers many powerful resources developed specifically for military marriages. In addition, this organization teams up with chaplains and other ministries to provide spiritual resources that troops and their families can draw upon during tough times.

http://www.samsonsociety.org
Samson Society is a fellowship of Christian men seeking friendship and discipleship. The site provides information for starting a group in your area.

notes

1. Lisa Belkin, "When Mom and Dad Share It All," *New York Times Magazine* (June 15, 2008), http://www.nytimes.com/z2008/06/15/magazine/15parenting-t.html?_r=3&oref=slog in&ref=magazine&pagewanted=all&oref=slogin (accessed May 1, 2009).

2. Dave Ridley, "The Company Built on Love" (speech, Workplace Leaders Forum, Dallas, October 27, 2008).

3. Visit www.familymanager.com to find out about working with a Family Manager Coach.

4. See http://teamnutrition.usda.gov/resources/mpk_tips.pdf. All informational materials produced by the USDA Center for Nutrition Policy and Promotion are in the public domain.

index

acknowledgments

Just as teamwork is critical to a family's success, it is critical to a book's success.

I count myself blessed to work with the wonderful team at Tyndale House: Mark Taylor, Doug Knox, Jan Long Harris, Kim Miller, Yolanda Sidney, Sarah Atkinson, Stephanie Voiland, Maggie Rowe, Mike Morrison, and Sharon Leavitt. Thank you all for your support, encouragement, and commitment to excellence.

Heartfelt thanks also go to two amazing women: Tyra Damm, for her editorial input (always outstanding, not to mention prompt) and for allowing me to use her family's story; and Nancy Lovell, a gifted wordsmith who can bring energy to the weariest of sentences. Their talent and expertise take my writing to the next level.

about kathy peel

Kathy Peel is called America's Family Manager by the media and millions of moms. She is the author of 21 books (over 2 million sold), including *Desperate Households* and *The Busy Mom's Guide to a Happy, Organized Home*, 2009 winner of the Mom's Choice Award for Best Family and Parenting Resource and a 2009 National Association of Parenting Publications honoree.

She is the founder and CEO of Family Manager. Her company equips and encourages women worldwide to build strong families and happy, organized homes (www.familymanager.com). She writes a weekly Family Manager blog for AOL's ParentDish, is AOL's Kids and Family Coach, and serves on the board of experts for *Parenting* magazine and InternetSafety.com. She writes a monthly column in *HomeLife* and is a regular contributor to *American Profile*. Her articles and tips have appeared in numerous publications, including *Real Simple*, *First for Women*, *Family Circle*, *Reader's Digest*, *Ladies' Home Journal*, and *Redbook*.

Kathy is frequently interviewed on TV and radio programs and has made repeat appearances on *The Oprah Winfrey Show*, *The Early Show*, *The Today Show*, CNN, HGTV, *The 700 Club*, *Focus on the Family*, Moody Radio's *Midday Connection*, and *Janet Parshall's America*. She is also a popular speaker at women's events, corporate programs, and church retreats.

"How can I reduce sibling bickering?"

"Can I plan a memorable birthday party without breaking the bank?"

"How do I display my faith in God to my children?"

WHEN BUSY MOMS HAVE QUESTIONS LIKE THESE, THEY NEED ANSWERS ...FAST!

Kathy Peel, America's Family Manager, offers quick solutions and practical advice in *The Busy Mom's Guide to a Happy, Organized Home*, an easy-access reference guide that covers all of the key questions asked by women who want to be the best moms possible. Containing a comprehensive index, helpful checklists and charts, and an extensive list of online resources, *The Busy Mom's Guide to a Happy, Organized Home* is the number one resource to guide moms from bewilderment and confusion to confidence and maturity as they perform the important job God has called them to do.

Restore order & harmony to your life & home ... starting today!

Feeling overwhelmed? It's time to turn to Kathy Peel, America's Family Manager, for help. In *Desperate Households*, Kathy offers realistic, do-it-today ways to complete your own life-changing household makeover and bring calm to your chaotic days. You'll learn about common scenarios that cause women the most stress; pinpoint what's driving your own anxiety; and discover personal, lasting solutions that will work for your family.

Make home your favorite place to be— and sweep desperation out the door!

desperate households

Features
10 LIFE-CHANGING FAMILY MANAGEMENT MAKEOVERS

kathy PEEL

Picket Fence Press

An inspiring collection of journeys down the paths of life . . .
for those who dream of a happy, well-managed home,
a place where you and your family long to be,
an atmosphere where your children can flourish and relationships deepen.

Come and join us . . .

as we discover new places, purposes, and hope for a balanced life,
learning secrets from other busy women,
nurturing our souls while stretching our faith,
and finding fulfillment in the important work we do every day.

Look for Picket Fence Press books, an imprint of Tyndale House Publishers,
everywhere books are sold.

A FAMILY MANAGER RESOURCE

Making home your favorite place to be

CP0125